P9-DUJ-972

# Trouble No More

▼ ▼ ▼

**_Stories by_**
**_Anthony Grooms_**

Palo Alto, California

Trouble No More



For information address La Questa Press,

555 Hamilton Avenue, Palo Alto, California 94301

Cover and text design by Kajun Graphics

Cover illustration by Hilary Mosberg

ISBN 0-9644348-0-6

Library of Congress Catalog Card Number: 95-67156

Second printing, 1996.

*To Robert Earl and Dellaphine Grooms*
*and Shannon and Mellinee Jackson*
*Yours was the generation of the great and little struggles*

*Special thanks to my wife Pamela Jackson*
*and to my friend, J.D. Scott, for their encouragement;*
*and to Kate Abbe for her hard work and faith.*

Grateful acknowledgement is made to the following publications for permisson to reprint previously published stories:

"Uncle Beasley's Courtship": *African American Review,* "Sweet Milton": *George Washington Review,* "The Lighthouse": *The Blue Plate Special,* "How I Got My Personal Politics" first appeared as "Mary's Awful Wig": *Catalyst,* "Negro Progress": *Callaloo.*



Work on this manuscript has been supported by The Georgia Council for the Arts, The Fulton County Commission for the Arts, and The City of Atlanta Bureau of Cultural Affairs.

Someday, Baby!
Ain't no trouble for me anymore
Trouble no more!

—*Muddy Waters*

# Contents

▼ ▼ ▼

# Uncle Beasley's Courtship

We were sitting in Momma's den waiting for Thanksgiving dinner when Daddy, against Momma's express orders, offered Uncle Beasley a highball. The next thing I knew, and it only took two downs on the TV screen, Uncle Beasley had gotten up from the La-Z-Boy, opened the cabinet and was making himself another one. He didn't do much mixing either, just poured some gin right over the ice and waddled back to his chair. He slapped down in the chair, slid forward a little, and turned toward me. His gray face was heavily wrinkled, and he pressed his chin into his neck and looked at me with his bulging eyes. "Boy," he said in a rough voice, "ain't you got nothing better'n me to look at?" I nodded and turned back to the TV. "When you been through what all I have," he said, and I looked around to see him rubbing his palm across his kinky, smoke-colored hair, "you deserve a drink or two."

"What you been through?" I asked.

"You don' wanna know. You couldn't appreciate it." He drank the gin like it was water and smacked his lips afterward. The sweet odor floated over to me, mixed with the smell of turkey and bread coming from the kitchen. I lay on my stomach, leaned on my elbows and looked up at him. "How can I appreciate it if you don' tell me what it is? If you tell me . . ."

He fumbled inside his ratty cardigan and took out a package of Camels. He put the glass on the coffee table, and I thought I ought to get a coaster from the table drawer. But I didn't move. I watched him slowly shake a cigarette from the package, and, with a slight tremble in his hand, place it on the edge of his lips. He searched himself again and then asked for matches.

"Momma don' like smoking in the house," I said.

He asked again for matches.

"Momma don' 'low smoking."

"You know what is your trouble, boy?"

"Ain't got one."

"Ain't knowed you got one."

"What is it then?"

He got up with the glass and went to the cabinet again. "You' momma. You' a momma's boy. Momma's boy ain't a man. Momma's boy a punk, and a punk don't get no poontang. If you don't get no poontang then you can't appreciate a man like me."

I started to ask what was poontang when he looked up from pouring and gave me a crafty, twinkling look, so that I knew he was waiting for me to ask.

"I get poontang when I want it," I said.

He was half grinning and waddled on back to the chair, stepping on the cuffs of his pants because they were falling off his hips. "That's how much you know. Poontang ain't no *it.* It's a she." He held the cigarette between his fingers like he was smoking it.

"What about her?"

He swallowed the gin and his eyes looked like they were about to spin, and it was just the sheer force of his grimace that held them still.

"Ain't none of your business," he said. "Ain't nobody's business but my own."

Momma came into the den undoing her apron and folding it up. Then she stopped and sniffed the air. "Uncle Beasley. Lord, Uncle Beasley, who let you into the liquor cabinet?"

Uncle Beasley smushed his chin up against his neck and looked over at me. He acted like he didn't hear Momma and Momma looked to me for an answer.

"Daddy told him."

"Bill," Momma called over her shoulder as she fussed over Uncle Beasley, trying to make him sit up straight. "Lord, Lord. Why didn't you wear that new sweater I gave you last Christmas, Uncle Beasley? Why do you let yourself go like this?" She was picking at his sweater and pushing his tie back into a knot. "Used to be you wouldn't be caught dead looking like this. Where's the uncle I used to know and love? Where's your pride, Uncle Beasley? Your pride?"

Uncle Beasley pushed Momma's hand away and sat up and started like he was straightening himself up. "I got my pride, girl, if I ain't got nothin' else."

Momma stood back and put her hands on her hips. "Well, you should look like it. You should try to keep yourself up. Why don't you go up and rinse your mouth before Miss Perkins gets here. She is a very respectable woman and I want things to go right."

The doorbell rang and we heard Daddy going for it. "Bill...," Momma called and started out of the room, but then stopped a second to order me to pick up the den and make myself look presentable.

Uncle Beasley looked at me and shook his head. His eyes were watery and he looked sweaty. "Ain't one damn man in this house," he said.

▼ ▼ ▼

Miss Perkins retired from principal at the school, but she still walked and talked like one, which was the main reason I wished Momma hadn't invited her. But Momma thought it would be good for Uncle Beasley to meet a woman friend his own age. I had to sit next to her at the table, with Daddy on my left at the head, Uncle Beasley at the foot next to Miss Perkins, and Momma on the other side next to the kitchen door. Momma served up the table, we prayed, and Daddy cut up the turkey and passed around the plates. Miss Perkins asked me what college I aspired to attend and in what I aspired to concentrate my studies. I told her I didn't know because I was just sixth grade. Momma said that wasn't a polite response, so I had to come up with a college, and since the Tide was playing on TV, I said Alabama and I said I had a great interest in math. Come to it, she was a math teacher before she became a principal, so I had to tell her what kind of math. "Calculations," I said. She smiled one of those ain't-he-cute smiles, and Momma said didn't I mean calculus. I didn't know what the hell calculus was and looked up at Daddy. But Daddy just had this dumb grin on his face, so I looked to Uncle Beasley. He was chewing very slowly, looking at Momma, then Miss Perkins, then me, then Miss Perkins and then me. He swallowed his food and took a sip of his water.

"Gerald," Momma said sternly. "You do mean calculus, don't you?"

Uncle Beasley looked at me, then he turned with a pleasant, still smile and said, "I bet you know everything there is to know about calculus, Miss Perkins, an intelligent, good-looking woman like you."

Miss Perkins patted her lips with the napkin and put it back in her lap with a flare. "Oh, Mr. Beasley. Do call me Gladys."

It was well known that Miss Perkins had been through two husbands already, but Momma said due to no fault of her own. Momma and Daddy had fussed about having her over for Thanksgiving. Daddy being of the opinion that she put on more airs than a flophouse queen.

A flophouse, he told me, was like a retirement home for show business people. Momma didn't take to that flophouse description. She said that Miss Perkins had just the kind of strict hand that Uncle Beasley needed. Besides Miss Perkins was the only church-going woman in all of Montgomery county that would be willing to sit with Uncle Beasley.

"Gladys," Uncle Beasley repeated. "What a lovely name. Almost as lovely as your person."

Momma had a smile on her face that made her mouth look frozen. "Isn't he a tease?" she said.

"He's a charmer," Miss Perkins said, like Uncle Beasley wasn't even there.

The rest of the supper wasn't so bad because Uncle Beasley had gotten me off the hook and now Miss Perkins was making little glances over at him and smiling. She and Momma talked about Negro progress and how far colored people had come in the last few years. Miss Perkins patted me on the back at one time and said that I was right to aspire to the University of Alabama because it was my home school, and due to brave people like Miss Autherine Lucy, I could go there if I wanted to and do just as well as those white children—only I would have to work twice as hard in order to get any credit for it. Then Momma puffed up real proud and told all about Uncle Beasley. She said that when he was going to college, to get around letting him go to Alabama, the state paid most of his way to New York University, which was a better education anyway. Uncle Beasley had majored in business administration and had his own real estate firm in Birmingham.

Miss Perkins said she hadn't known about that, but she had heard about his insurance dealings in Montgomery and his wonderful contributions to colored progress in our city. He was a real credit, and she had always wanted to meet him. Momma said how Uncle Beasley always helped the colored folks, even if it meant he made less money or couldn't buy a fancy car like the white insurance men. He did right, Miss Perkins said, because if Negroes didn't look out for Negroes, nobody else would.

While they talked about him, Uncle Beasley just ate steadily and ignored them. And when they finished he smiled at Miss Perkins and said, "I always enjoy meeting prominent young ladies like yourself."

Miss Perkins put the napkin to her bosom, which was very large and protruded right up to the edge of the table. "Why, thank you, Beasley—I may call you Beasley? It is always nice to be called young."

"I like young women," Uncle Beasley said. "The younger the better."

Momma suddenly lifted her chair back from the table and said dessert was served, and Daddy and me had to gobble down our seconds and clear the table. She brought in plates of sweet-potato pie and ice cream, and Uncle Beasley said he didn't want one. He said he had enough sweetness just looking at Miss Perkins. Miss Perkins put her fingers to her mouth like she was surprised and batted her eyes at Uncle Beasley. Momma cleared her throat and told Uncle Beasley that Miss Perkins was our *guest* and that the dinner table was not the right place for fool talk. She looked at Daddy. "Isn't that right, Bill?"

"Pie's mighty good," Daddy said. "Mighty good."

Uncle Beasley looked at Daddy, then me, then Miss Perkins and then took a long, hard look at Momma. Momma turned and smiled to Miss Perkins and started to say where she had gotten the potatoes to make the pie.

"Ain't no fool talk," Uncle Beasley interrupted. He scooted back his chair on the hardwood floor with a screech that made Momma grimace and excused himself.

"He's very sensitive," Momma said. "You know, since his business troubles."

Miss Perkins said she had heard about Uncle Beasley's troubles and it was a great shame that a man of his stature . . .

"Shame is right." Momma cleared her throat and nodded toward me to tell Miss Perkins she didn't want to talk in front of me, so I knew they weren't just talking about business. I looked up at Daddy. He gave me a wink and asked me who had won the football game.

▼ ▼ ▼

After supper Momma told me and Daddy that we could wash the dishes later and to retire to the den so that we could converse with our guests. I would rather have washed the dishes, because I knew Momma wasn't going to let me watch TV, and I would have to sit up straight and listen while she and Miss Perkins talked about the school board and all the goings-on between the teachers and the white and colored; or she would talk about her specialty, home economics, and how young women were ruining themselves—not to mention shaming the race—by not paying more attention to her in class. But when I got in there I sat right across from Uncle Beasley, who was slumped on the sofa with another glass of ice and gin and was slowly sipping and looking glum. Momma pushed a pillow around him like she was trying to make him more comfortable, but she was really trying to get him to sit up straight without Miss Perkins catching on. Momma offered Miss Perkins the La-Z-Boy, but Miss Perkins said that she thought she would be more comfortable on the sofa and that Daddy ought to have the La-Z-Boy anyway. That was really a man's chair, she said. Momma told her to make herself at home, but she gave Daddy this look like there was no telling what would happen next. Then she offered Miss Perkins a highball and set about making everybody a drink, except me and Uncle Beasley.

"What you think about ole Nixon?" Daddy started in on his favorite subject which was politics.

"Oh, Bill," Momma said, "nobody wants to talk about the election. What's done is done."

Uncle Beasley cleared his throat. “Ain’t nothin’ done if it’s kicking.”

“Why, Beasley, whatever do you mean by that?” Miss Perkins took her drink from Momma and turned her knees toward Uncle Beasley. “You don’t think it’s too late for a recount?”

“Never count a man out ‘til he’s dead and gone.” Uncle Beasley started fumbling in his sweater for a cigarette.

“I’m mighty afraid that Humphrey’s gone.” Daddy leaned back in the chair and took a deep breath and I could tell he was swelling up for a long speech.

“I ain’t talking about Humphries.” Uncle Beasley found the cigarette and put it on his lips. “I’m talking about a man.” He fumbled again and stopped and told me to go get a match. I looked at Momma, who was looking at Daddy, who was looking at Uncle Beasley. Then Uncle Beasley turned to Miss Perkins. “What do you think, Gladys? You think a man ought to just lay up like a lazy dog just because he got knocked down once or twice?”

“Why, Mr. Beasley, I…”

“Well, would you want a man like that?”

“I’ve never given it much thought, I…”

“I b’leve you’ve been giving it a lot of thought. I b’leve you thinking about it right now.”

“Uncle Beasley!” Momma said.

“Oh, no,” Miss Perkins stopped Momma with a wag of her finger. “I’ve been a high school principal long enough to know how to handle fresh young boys.”

“I ain’t a boy. And I don’t see how you can look at me and call me one.”

“But you’re acting like one,” Momma said.

“I’m acting like what I *is*. I’m acting just like what you see in front of you.”

Miss Perkins stuck out her chest. "All I see is a charming old drunkard."

Uncle Beasley straightened himself up and rested his glass on his knee. In a quick, thoughtful movement he snatched the cigarette from his lips. "Miss Perkins," he started slowly, "you' a nice lady. You' a learned lady and you've made a great contribution to the community. But you don't know everything there is to know, leastwise you don't know all there is to know about me."

"Well, what is there to know?" Momma laughed, trying to cut him off.

"Louise. You my sister's only child, and I know you mean well. But why don't you shut your flap for now and let me have my say."

"Bill."

Daddy looked at Momma and then turned to Uncle Beasley and asked if he could fill his glass again. Uncle Beasley smiled and turned back to Miss Perkins. "Gladys, let me tell you a story that will give you a little history about me. I never took time to get married. Was always too busy with this deal or that one, making money and trying to make something of myself. I was trying to be a credit to my race, and I'll say I did my share. But then one morning I looked at myself and what I saw was a old gray-haired man who was heading out to a dingy old office up in Pleasant Hill, where I'd write policies and buy and sell and make good money and come home to an empty house. On holidays where would I go but over to my niece's house and spend the time with her family, 'cause I didn't have one of my own. No offense. I love my niece, but it ain't the same as having your own. Then come a young woman, young enough to be my daughter. Come in for me to write her a policy. And I did. I asked her questions about her life, was she married, who her parents were—the standard questions—and the more I asked, the more I saw myself leaning in toward her and wishing for her, not just for sex—" he shot a glance at Momma to quiet her— "I wanted companionship—though sex was OK too."

"I hardly think it's appropriate to discuss your affairs," Miss Perkins said and looked at Momma like she was embarrassed.

"Why not?" said Uncle Beasley. "You been doing it behind my back, ain't you? Ain't that part of the reason you come over here today? To see the old fool in person? The old fool that run after the young gal and lost all his money to her?"

Miss Perkins craned her neck and opened her mouth to speak. But Uncle Beasley wouldn't let her. He used the sofa arm to pull himself to the edge of the sofa seat. "I appreciate it that Louise thought enough of me to gossip. And that's what it was to you." He rubbed his hand across his head. "But to me it was my first sweet love. I was sixty-two years old, but I was a schoolboy. My feet didn't touch the ground for two years. Every time I saw that girl a-coming, my heart stopped beating and my mind went fuzzy. I couldn't concentrate on my business, and money just poured out of my pockets like water out of a faucet. But do you think I cared one iota? No. Not a hellish iota. Because I was in love. I didn't care about the cars I bought her, or the clothes and coats, and clubs and trips to New York City. You name it, we done it. She ruined me. But you know what I'm thinking right now?" He looked at Momma, and Momma turned her face away. "Right now?" He put the cigarette back on his lips and patted himself for matches, then took the cigarette away. "Right now, I wish I was about that boy's age." He pointed at me with the hand that held the cigarette. "Then I would start out all over again. I would change everything. I wouldn't care about business, or progress or education. Just one thing."

"You wouldn't *say it.* Momma stood up straight as board. "You wouldn't *say it* in my house."

Everybody was still and quiet for a moment, with Momma straight and tense and glaring down at Uncle Beasley, and Uncle Beasley sitting so close to the edge of the sofa he was more squatting than sitting. Then he relaxed and sat back. "No, child. It *is* your house. Yours and Bill's. And I know when I done said enough."

I couldn't figure out what it was he couldn't say in front of Momma; there were so many things Momma wouldn't let you say. But I had never seen Momma this stiff, so stiff she was standing on her toes, which I didn't realize until she relaxed a little and her heels slid back into her shoes. I looked at Daddy to see if he would give me a clue. He was looking down at his highball and swirling the ice cubes around. Miss Perkins had her napkin to her lips, looking like she was wrestling down a belch. I figured it must have been the name of the girl that Uncle Beasley couldn't say. She must have been one of them fresh girls—womanish girls—as Momma called them, who made trouble in high school and went on dates with boys that wasn't even in high school. Maybe she had been one of Momma's students. Maybe that was why he couldn't say her name. Her name started to swell up inside me, and I squeezed my knees together to keep it down.

Then Momma turned to me, patting her hair. "Gerald, why don't you run and get a head start on the dishes, and Daddy will come to help you later." She threw a little smile behind it, but her eyes sparkled she was so mad. I got up right away like I had been taught to obey, but what Uncle Beasley had said about there not being no man in the house gave me a tug. I knew she was my momma and all and I loved her, but I didn't think it was fair that she wouldn't even let Uncle Beasley say his girlfriend's name in the house—and Daddy sitting over there playing with his ice cubes. I had started on the steps that go down to the split-level when I ran back, half stumbling, the word tripping me up.

"Gerald?" Momma said and everybody looked at me, and I felt my mouth open and shut like a goldfish that done hopped out the bowl.

"Gerald?" Momma's voice went up a little like she thought I was sick or something, and then, before I much knew it, it came out of me like a shout of relief.

"Poontang! Right? That her name? Poontang!"

Miss Perkins' napkin stopped about six inches from her mouth, and Daddy stopped swirling his glass but his ice kept going around. They looked at me and then at Momma, and I looked at Uncle Beasley, who was sitting just looking like he hadn't heard a thing.

"What did you say?" Momma asked in that tone that told me I had better not answer because she had heard me plain enough and was just asking to see how bad a trouble I wanted. It was something about Uncle Beasley, the way he was slumped on the sofa, like his spine had turned to mashed potatoes. So I turned to Momma, and I wasn't mean at all, and I said, "Her name? Ain't it Poontang?"

Momma sighed and folded her arms and acted like she was relaxed. "Young man, where did you learn a word like that?" It was then that I realized that it was not just a name, but one of those words that adults were always saying, but punishing children for saying. The way Momma looked at me, I knew I had made a bad mistake. It seemed obvious that she knew who had told the name to me. She wanted to get at Uncle Beasley. If I told her he had told it to me, she would just give me a talk, or tell Daddy to do it, and send me on out to wash the dishes. Then she would have a time with Uncle Beasley. I looked at Uncle Beasley slumped down with his chin against his chest and his pudgy stomach showing through his shirt, and I knew I couldn't say who told me.

"Didn't you hear me *speak* to you?" Momma barely parted her teeth when she spoke and her jawbone was twitching besides. She shot a glance at Uncle Beasley, then back to me. "Come here."

I fumbled a moment, trying to come up with something to say, and looked around for somebody to help me. Daddy was sitting up straight in his chair and looking at Momma like he was waiting for her to give him his turn. Miss Perkins had folded her napkin in her lap and picked up an *Ebony* magazine and was staring down at the cover.

"I *said* come here."

I shuffled over, just a foot or two, but close enough.

"Where did you learn that filthy word?"

She didn't really want me to answer, because when I opened my mouth to say I didn't know it was a bad word, she walloped me across the mouth with her open palm. My eyes watered up and my nose ran and I ran my tongue over my lips thinking I would taste blood.

"Now, *sir,* apologize to our guests." She grabbed me roughly by the shoulders and spun me around to face Miss Perkins. "Apologize!"

My lips felt so thick that I could hardly get them apart to say anything, but I managed to say, "I apologize."

Miss Perkins looked up from the magazine like she was surprised, and she said, "Apology accepted."

My face was burning now, not just from the slap but from the way Miss Perkins was looking at me, so coy, but I could see she was dying to get a good laugh out of it. I started toward the stairs, but Momma stopped me.

"Sir. Where do you think you're going? I said apologize to our guests."

"I did."

"You didn't to Uncle Beasley. He is a guest in this house."

Uncle Beasley looked up at me through his slitted eyelids, his face red and shiny. I thought, He wouldn't let me apologize to him; he told me the word. He pushed himself up straight and I thought now he would say something to Momma, tell her it wasn't my fault that I had said the damn word. But he just sat there and folded his arms across his chest like he was preparing himself to hear my apology. I thought, Well, maybe he was playing it out for Momma and that he would give me a wink, some little sign to let me know that he knew it wasn't my fault and that this was something that would be kept between men. But no wink came. Instead, Momma's hand came and whacked the back of my head, making me duck and hold my face.

"What did I tell you to do?" she said.

Daddy stood up and I knew that Momma had given him the signal to give me the belt. If Uncle Beasley would only give me a little sign, like tell me it was a secret joke, then I could apologize, but his face had this expectant look on it, worse than Miss Perkins, because he was acting sanctimonious, and I could have kicked him as soon as open my mouth to him.

"Did you hear your momma?" Daddy asked in the way he was obliged to.

I didn't say anything. Just breathed hard. The room filled up with my breathing and I wished I was breathing out arms with hands with long fingers that would float over and choke Uncle Beasley.

"Son?" Daddy's voice was soft, half-begging, because he didn't like to whip and I was building fast to a whipping. Then Momma shoved me toward him, and that was the sign to whip. But I stepped right back in front of Uncle Beasley so he would know that I blamed him for it. He was looking straight at me, but his face held that sanctimonious expression like he just couldn't understand what devil had gotten into me.

▼ ▼ ▼

All during the whipping I thought about that look on Uncle Beasley's face. I lay across my bed sideways with my pants around my ankles and Daddy laying leather to my bare butt. Daddy was an easy whipper when Momma wasn't around, and she had stayed in the den with the guests. All I had to do was to whimper a little and he would call it quits. I just clutched at the bedspread each time that belt stung across my buttocks, but I didn't even breathe hard. He could beat me all night if he wanted to. He could beat me until I died, at least I would die a man.

Finally Daddy stopped and he said, "Son?" but I didn't say a thing. He sat on the bed beside me, and I thought he was going to deliver one of his pep talks, but he didn't say anything, just sat quiet awhile. We could hear Momma in the den telling Miss Perkins she didn't know what on earth had possessed me, and Miss Perkins finally getting her laugh in.

Not until Daddy left did I pull up my pants, and then I lay across the bed in the dark and listened to the grown-ups talk and finally say good night. I heard Momma helping Daddy in the kitchen and then they went to bed. Way into the night, I got up and went into the kitchen to get a drink of water. On the way, I saw Uncle Beasley still sitting on the couch where he had been. He was slumped down and looking straight ahead, his eyes half open and still. I stood looking at him, thinking now would be a good time to put a pillow over his face, when it occurred to me that he might already be dead. I couldn't see him breathing and he was as still as a picture.

Then without moving a muscle, he suddenly said, "What you looking at, boy?"

I tried to cover up being startled by saying, just as mean as I could, "You, that's who."

"Ain't you got something better to do than look at an old fool?"

"Maybe I like looking at old fools."

He rubbed his palms across his face. "You live long enough, boy, you see a lot a fools. Old ones, and young ones, too."

# Negro Progress

The water hunted the boy. It chipped bark from the oaks as he darted behind the trees. It caught him in the back. His lanky legs buckled. Then, as if the fireman who directed the hose were playing a game, the boy's legs were cut from under him, and he was rolled over and over in the mud.

From the distance of half a block, Carlton Wilkes watched the white ropes of water as they played against the black trunks and lime-green leaves of the trees. In the sunlight, the streams sparkled, occasionally crisscrossed or made lazy S's.

He had been on his way to his Uncle Booker's building when he first saw the children. They were wearing school clothes. He remembered that somebody in King's organization had called for a children's crusade, placing teenagers and children as young as six on the front lines of the city's civil rights demonstrations. Even when the first fire truck skidded to a stop across the street from the park and the firemen unwound their hoses and screwed them into the hydrants, he paid little attention. Uncle Booker had quite literally ordered him downtown. "It's only your damn future that's at stake," he had said. Uncle Booker had a way of exaggerating, but when it came to business, his feet were flat on the ground. There was little Negro business that went on in the city that Uncle Booker didn't have a hand in.

Then a child's squeal, the squeal and the whoosh-and-scour of the water, made him look up at the sometimes taut, sometimes lazy ropes the firemen directed. At first, the children taunted the firemen. They danced about, darting under the arcing streams and through the mist of the pressurized water. Then the boy was tripped and rolled with such force that Carlton thought he must have been hurt. He told himself to move, to run to the boy, but this meant passing the fire trucks. Then he saw the paddy wagons and the handsome German shepherds. His legs went rubbery.

▼ ▼ ▼

His legs seemed barely strong enough to push in the clutch as he drove to Salena's house. He and Salena Parrish had been engaged for six months but had not set a date for the wedding. She was a nurse at the city hospital, one of the first Negro nurses there. When she opened the door he saw in her expression how harried he looked.

"What happened to you?" she asked, her gray eyes growing wide for a second.

The sight of her made his heart rush. Her light skin blushed in response to his breathlessness. He stumbled across the threshold, stammering. Not until she had taken him by the shoulders did he manage to speak.

"They...they are *hosing* children—shooting them down like...like the Boston massacre."

For a moment she looked horrified, then seemed to understand him and relaxed a little. "You mean *spraying* them with water?" She tightened the belt on her robe and turned on the radio. "Just *hosing* them with water?"

There was no news on the radio. She led him to the sofa, spoke soothingly to him, and brought him a drink. It was cheap whiskey, but it calmed him. She took his hand and asked him to tell her what had happened.

"Let me get another drink." He went to the decanter in the dining room. The decanter was made of gaudy cut glass. He poured a finger, swallowed it, and poured another. The trembling stopped; he felt a little more like himself. "Doesn't your old man ever buy good liquor?"

"You know it's only for display."

He talked a moment about what he had seen, but when he got to the part about rescuing the boy, he stopped.

"Then what did you do?" She leaned toward him.

He sipped the whiskey. "I came here."

"What happened to the boy?"

"I don't know."

"Well," she said and sat back on the sofa. "Probably nothing. The radio hasn't said a thing."

The trembling came back. He paced. "I just don't know. I have a sick feeling. I can't explain it. It feels like…like my whole insides want to come out." He stopped while she took the curler out of her bangs. "It feels like something bad is going to happen, and if I stay here—I mean if *we*—stay here we are going to be trapped in it."

"Well, there *is* a civil rights protest."

He took a breath. "Don't be sarcastic."

"I don't mean to be sarcastic. I'm just pointing out to you that something *is* happening. You don't realize it because you don't see it every day. And, well, you have options those people don't have. Money gives you options."

"What is that supposed to mean?"

"Just an observation." Then she added quickly, "Not of you—not so much of you, sweetheart—but of my patients. You feel you may get trapped. You can afford to go to New York or California. But most of them can't. At least not in the way I'm talking about."

"What's the difference in New York?" He closed his eyes. "I wish I could really get away from here. From this city. From the whole damn country." He sat on the sofa and took her hand. "I'm serious. Why don't we get married and go overseas? We could go to Amsterdam or Paris. I hear things aren't so bad over there."

"Paris? Oh sure, *mon cher.* And just what are we going to do in *Paris?* We don't have that kind of money."

"I'll sell Dad's part of the business to Uncle Booker. He buys up everything sooner or later anyway."

"He *is* a businessman."

Carlton remembered his meeting with his uncle. "And I'm not?"

▼ ▼ ▼

He did not go right away to meet his uncle. Salena decided to go to the hospital and asked him to make lunch for her father. Her father, Mr. Parrish, was a wiry, olive man with patchy gray fuzz on his head. He seemed agitated when he came in from his store and found Carlton in the kitchen warming up string beans and leftover turkey. "Where's Salena, Mr. Wilkes? She done got called in?"

"She went in before they called her."

"Volunteered her time? She know better'n that."

"I believe she felt they would call her anyway with the riot going on downtown."

"Riot?" He went to the washroom just off the kitchen. "I ain't hear tell of no riot. Heard they spraying them children. But spraying ain't a riot."

"No, sir. I guess not." Carlton watched Mr. Parrish's angular hips as he bent over the basin. "Anyway, Salena asked me to warm up some dinner for you." He poured the limp, sweet-smelling beans onto the plate with the turkey and candied yams. His stomach growled a little, but he decided not to eat until the old man invited him.

Mr. Parrish put the paper napkin to his collar and began his lunch. "You not in business today?"

"I had an appointment down with Uncle Booker, but...the disturbance was in the way."

"That's what I knew. They talk about hurtin' the white man, but they hurtin' the colored, too." Mr. Parrish sawed on his turkey. "Shuttlesworth and Walker! Call themselves preachers. Preachers ain't got no business in politics, if you ask me. Marchin' in the street ain't never got nobody into heaven." He motioned with the fork to a chair. "Help yourself, Carlton."

"I'm not very hungry."

"Can't work if you don't eat. That's what my daddy always told me. He was a farming man. Worked me sunup 'til midnight. I ain't lying. He was born a slave, you know. Had that slave working mentality. Nothing wrong with a work mentality. Two things I swore when I was a boy. One: I would get ahead any way I could—but ain't but one way—hard work. After my daddy died, Momma moved us over here to live with her brother who worked at the furnace. That when I saw how to make it: business. Momma opened the little dry goods store—just a handful of inventory—and I carried it on. My brother, Tom, he went back to farming—still farming—don't own a thing. Ain't got no pension. No nothing."

Carlton wiped sweat from his forehead back into his hair. He was wishing for a drink and the smell of the turkey was making him hungry. "What was the second thing?"

"I'll get to it." Mr. Parrish chewed. "Farming. That's what. Never gone lift another hoe in my life—unless it is to sell it. That's what your average Negro don't understand. He go out, break his back, whether it's farmin' or minin' or smeltin'—and ain't got a red cent to show for it. You got to be the middleman. The middleman or the owner. It's still hard work, but you got something in the end. Something you can sell if nothing else." He drank water. "Take yourself. You still young. You and Salena both. Well, she doing the best she can for a woman, but nursing—first colored girl or not—that's not what I want for her. She needs to settle in and raise the children and take care of the house. It's nice she got a skill and all to lean back on, in case something happens to you." He winked. "That's one thing that worries me so much about this going on. Interferes with business. White and colored, too."

"Mr. Parrish, did you *see* what was going on downtown?"

"I heard they was spraying children. Children ought to be in school, not the street—how do they ever expect to get a job out in the street? I wouldn't hire nay one of 'em—and what do they expect a white man to say if they have this on their record...?"

"They were not spraying them. They were *hosing* them."

"What's the difference, Carlton?" Mr. Parrish stopped sawing the turkey with his fork. "What's the difference for us? It ain't fixin' to do nothin' but hurt us, one way or the other. Colored people too impatient. They want something and don't know what they gettin'. Now you tell me what sense it make for me to want to go all the way downtown and sit in at a white lunch counter to eat a hamburger, when my friend Harvey Brown got a rib shack not three blocks from here. And in your own business, Carlton, what good it gone be if they let us live up in Mountain Brook? You can't sell no houses in Mountain Brook, and ain't no white ever gone buy a house in Titusville. People talkin' about gettin' their freedom. Freedom ain't worth a dime if you ain't got a dime." He punched the table with his finger. "Every dollar they spend with the white man is a dollar they ain't spent with us." He pushed back from the table and folded his arms. "We got to think this thing through. This marching business liable to drive every colored man in the city out of business."

The two men sat quietly for a moment as if considering this proclamation. Then Carlton shifted and cleared his throat. "Mr. Parrish, Salena and I have been talking. We figure if things don't get better we might go away."

The old man didn't look up. "Where to? Up North? Colored got the same trouble up North, only difference is they don't know it."

"We were thinking about Europe, maybe Paris."

"Paris, France?" Mr. Parrish looked at Carlton with incredulity. "You don't mean Paris, Kentucky? You mean Paris that in France? What the *hell* you going to do in Paris, France? You speak French? You got any family in France?" He sighed. "Son, white man own Paris just like he own Birmingham. Ain't a place in the world you can go—unlessen it's Red China—that the white man don't own. You can even go back to Africa, and you still got to deal with the white man. So you might as well save yo'self some running and deal with him right here."

▼ ▼ ▼

Uncle Booker kept him waiting. From the window in the outer office he could see the park. It showed no evidence of the disturbance. The intercom buzzed.

"Mr. Wilkes," the secretary called to him. "He will see you now." Just before she opened the door for him, she whispered in a matronly way, "Straighten your tie."

Uncle Booker looked at his watch and shook his head.

"I was here on time, Uncle Booker. But there was a riot."

"You let that foolishness stop you?"

"It was more than just a little foolishness." Carlton walked quickly to the window. "Didn't you see it from here?"

"I saw it. But I didn't let it get in the way of what I had to do." Uncle Booker packed and lit his pipe. "Have a seat, son. Believe it or not, I was young once, so I know how it is to get excited about things that don't mean a difference to you one way or the other."

"But..."

"I know. I know." Booker waved him silent with a chubby hand. "You're concerned about your rights—about Negro progress—I'm for all that, too. Lord, I'd be a fool not to be. And believe me, sure as the sun comes up every morning, it's coming. Maybe these schoolchildren have started something. Maybe not. Maybe we'll be singing their praises or maybe we'll be burying them. Or maybe both." He puffed and swiveled in his chair. "And you got a part in this progress too."

Carlton's stomach churned. He couldn't see himself marching.

Booker put his pipe in the pipe rest. "This will sound awful hard, but it's the truth. For someone like you, educated up North and in a white school—and got a little money behind you—the only Negro progress is to make as much money as you can. Now, before you say anything stupid, let me remind you that for three generations, even before the end of slavery, the Wilkes family has been in one business or the other. We may not have gotten our rights from the white man, and damn it, I know we didn't get his respect, but we got what we wanted because we had money."

Carlton had heard it before. Uncle Booker recounted the Wilkes businesses, from the small farm and produce store his first free ancestor had, to the white-only barbershops Carlton's grandfather had owned, to the real estate company that Carlton's father had owned, and to Booker's own insurance company. Carlton studied the short, chubby man. It was hard to believe that he was related to him.

"Now, I have a deal for you," Booker continued. "It should make you and your lady very happy—and rich. There is a man, a Northerner—and I may add, a white man—who is proposing to build some stores in various places around the city. Mountain Brook will be the first one. These are what they call *convenience* stores. They'd sell sundries and quick items. This man needs a partner—an investor. Someone who knows the area, but yet isn't exactly one of the local Okies, if you catch my drift."

After a moment, Carlton spoke. "That would take a lot of money."

"You've got it. You'll need to sell off some of those slum houses your daddy left you, and it would be tight for a few years. But you're young, and you've got your young lady to fall back on. She's Parrish's only child, and you'll have what he leaves her. But the best part," he puffed on the pipe, "the very best part will be if this civil rights thing goes through, then you'll own property in Mountain Brook and black and white alike will already be buying from you."

Uncle Booker leaned back in his swivel chair and laid his intertwined fingers across his stomach. He seemed to have been caught in a daydream. Carlton went to the window again and looked out over the park. He remembered how he felt when he had seen the dogs, and turned quickly to Uncle Booker. "I don't know about going into business with a white man. People around here wouldn't like that. It could cause trouble." The mention of "trouble" was strategic. Trouble would be bad for business.

Uncle Booker leaned forward. "Nobody will know who owns what." He leaned back in the chair and frowned. "What's the matter with you, Carlton?"

"It's just that Salena and I had been thinking of leaving Birmingham. You know, going to someplace where we could get a good start."

"Like where?"

"Like Paris."

Uncle Booker's face was still for a moment, then he laughed. "How romantic!" He leaned forward and put his thick hands on the desktop.

"Son, what do you see when you look out that window at Birmingham? Filthy smokestacks? A shabby little downtown? For certain it is not Paris. What I see is a town that black people helped to build. I see opportunity on every street corner. *Your* opportunity. You can't be afraid to claim it."

Carlton looked out the window again. In the distance he saw the columns of white smoke rising from the steel furnaces in Hueytown. Hueytown was home to the KKK. In another direction, he saw the rooftops of Titusville. Only last week bombs had been tossed into houses in Titusville. Then there was the park just in front of him. He returned to his seat. How could he make Uncle Booker understand? "Everything is changing here."

"Change can be good."

"It's just that…I'm afraid."

Uncle Booker leaned back again. He put the pipe in his mouth. "Of course, there is some risk. If you want to make money, you've got to take risks."

"It's not the business, Uncle Booker. I'm afraid. Afraid of what's happening here."

"Afraid?" Uncle Booker frowned and rocked forward abruptly. "Afraid? Afraid to make money?"

▼ ▼ ▼

Carlton had started home after his talk with Uncle Booker, but the sight of the park stopped him. Close up, he could see the scars the water had left on the tree trunks and where it had stripped the leaves from shrubs. Here and there were puddles in the grass. He stood at the place where the boy had fallen. The grass was thin, and the ground had been churned up by running feet. It smelled fresh.

Remembering again what he had witnessed, he felt himself begin to shake. He looked at his hand. On the outside he was perfectly still, but on the inside everything trembled. He knew it was fear, but what did he have to fear?

Uncle Booker was right. He had nothing to lose if he played it smart. Money gave him options. He could invest and become very rich. The boycotts wouldn't hurt him. Or he could go to Europe. He couldn't live like a king in Europe, but he could live well for a long time.

He looked up from his hands and saw a police car circling the block. In the back, heads against the window, were two dogs.

▼ ▼ ▼

No one had answered at Salena's, and he had started back to his car when he saw the men gathering on a neighbor's porch. Mr. Shannon, the neighbor, waved. He was carrying a hunting rifle. Several of the half dozen or so men carried guns. The three shots of good bourbon he had had on the way over kept Carlton's stomach still.

Mr. Shannon, a tall, brown man with a wide mouth, beckoned to him. "It's about to come on."

Carlton straightened his tie. "What's that, Mr. Shannon?"

"Walter Cronkite."

Mrs. Shannon opened the window from the inside and pushed the television to face the men. Walter Cronkite appeared inside the oval screen and spoke about Birmingham. Then pictures of the hosing came up. Carlton saw the lanky silhouettes of the children, dancing about in the white mist. A jet smacked a child and tossed her down.

"God," one of the men said.

The whole newscast was about Birmingham. No one made a sound. Even when the governor made a defiant speech no one said a thing, though Carlton could see Mr. Shannon's forearms tighten. When the newscast ended, the men looked at each other, their jaws set in anger and their fists twisted around the barrels of the guns.

"The Klan will be out tonight," one of them said.

"I'd like to see them," another said.

Mr. Shannon relaxed a little. "I don't reckon so. I reckon they're at home watching it like we are. But we'd better be on guard anyway."

"Any hooded bastard come sneaking around this neighborhood, I get me a piece of 'm," a man said.

"All you do is give Pooler a piece of mortuary business."

"Now, gentlemen," Mr. Shannon said, "we got a higher cause than to talk like that." He turned to Carlton. "Mr. Wilkes, won't you join us on watch tonight? Ever since the bombings started, we sit on different porches to see if we can't discourage whoever is doing it."

They looked like an unlikely militia—schoolteachers, millworkers, and brickmasons, fidgeting with their shotguns and hunting rifles. Someone dropped a shell and it rolled and stopped at Carlton's feet. His hand trembled as he picked it up and held it out to its owner. He worried that they would think he was afraid.

"How about it, Mr. Wilkes?" Mr. Shannon asked.

Carlton cleared his throat. "No. Not tonight."

"When?" Mr. Shannon looked directly at him but spoke softly. "Comes a time when enough's enough, and you got to do what you got to do. I say when the fire department that I pay my taxes to go and hose little colored girls, then the time's come."

"Amen," someone said.

"Shannon's the next Martin Luther King," another man said and provoked laughter from the group.

Carlton's throat was dry. "I was there this morning, Mr. Shannon. I saw it." The men grunted sympathetically. "What you saw on television, I saw face-to-face."

"Then you know what I'm talking about." Mr. Shannon held out his gun to Carlton. "I got another gun in the house. Besides, we'll take turns carrying the guns."

"No. I...I wouldn't know how to use a gun."

"Just carry it like you know how," someone chimed in.

Carlton backed down the stairs. "I'm sorry, gentlemen, I have an appointment—across town, and I..."

"He's G. W. Parrish's son-in-law," one of them said. "He's too worried about business to be free."

"No call for that," Mr. Shannon said. "If the man's got business to do, then he's got business to do. He said he would join us another night."

"May not be another night."

One of the men made a joke. "One Wilkes'll rent you a house; the other one will insure it; Parrish'll sell you your stock; and Pooler will put you under, but nay one of 'em will fight for you." A stiff laugh came from the man who said it, a big, buck-toothed man Carlton knew as a brickmason. The other men only stared at Carlton, challenging him. He fumbled for an answer but realized it was no good. He couldn't stay with them now, even if he wanted to, but to run would make him a coward or, worse, a traitor.

Then a little girl, about five, a fragile, wide-eyed child with two erect plaits, came to the screen door. "Daddy," she called in a soft, quavering voice, "Daddy, are we going to get bombed tonight?"

Mr. Shannon opened the door, took his daughter into one arm, and wedged the rifle in the crook of the other. "No, honey, we ain't gonna get bombed."

▼ ▼ ▼

Carlton drove aimlessly until after sunset. The police were setting up checkpoints, so he drove back to Titusville and waited around the corner for Salena to get home from her shift. Soon after midnight, he saw her park her car in the driveway, nod to the men on Shannon's porch, and go quickly up the stairs. He caught up to her just before she shut the door.

"You scared me," she said. "God, Carlton, you've been drinking."

"I've been thinking."

"Come in before you wake up the neighborhood. And for God's sake, don't wake up Papa."

Carlton sat on the couch while Salena put away her things. She came back wearing her uniform and no shoes. "Listen. Maybe you should go. Daddy will have a fit if we keep him up on a work night."

A little dizzy from the drinking, Carlton stood. "I just wanted to say…" She pulled the pins out of her nurse's hat. In the dim overhead light her features were sullen. "I wish we could listen to music," he said.

"Papa'll…"

"I know what he'd do, but—don't you feel like you're between a rock and a hard place?"

She seemed to think for a moment. "No. What do you mean? I feel very lucky, altogether. Very lucky."

"You want to be more than just lucky. Never mind. I…"

He put his palm to his head and sighed. "I'm an ass."

She said nothing, but took his elbow and pushed him back to the sofa. "What's on your mind?"

It took him a moment to prevent his voice from cracking. "I want to get away. I'm scared this thing is going to backfire."

She folded her hands around his. "We had a fairly quiet night at the hospital. Mostly white. They were scared, too. Scared of the 'race riot.' One old woman said it was Armageddon. But when I saw those pictures of the children on the TV, I was *proud.* I don't know what will happen to them. I don't think it'll be good, but at least they aren't letting the white people get away with it—I mean, they are at least standing up for something." She took off her hat. Her hair fell down on her neck and she pulled it back and set it with the bobby pin.

"You weren't scared?" he whispered.

"A little. Who wouldn't be? But you've got to go on with your work."

"What about Paris?"

She sighed. "I guess I could be a nurse in Paris. The question is, what are *you* going to do?"

He took a flask from his jacket.

"Don't. It's too late. You've got to work tomorrow, don't you?"

Hearing Mr. Parrish on the stairs, Carlton put the flask away.

"Let me see if I can't send him back to bed." Salena went to the foot of the stairs and called to her father, telling him nothing was the matter. The old man complained about his interrupted sleep and kept coming down. Reluctantly, Carlton started toward the door.

"Mr. Wilkes," Mr. Parrish blurted. "What brings you around at this hour?" He was wearing a dingy sleeveless undershirt and trousers. "Something wrong downtown?"

"Everything is fine, Papa."

"Them children up to something?"

Salena tried to turn her father around at the foot of the stairs, but he brushed past her, eclipsed Carlton on the way to the door, and looked out of the sidelight. "Shannon and his crew still sittin' up. Waiting for the Ku Klux Klan!" He faced Carlton. His age showed in the bags and spots under his eyes. "Tell you one thing, the Klan ain't waitin' for them. They in bed gettin' their rest so they can put in a full day. Klan gone strike, he go 'head and strike and then go home and get a full night. Ain't that right, Mr. Wilkes?" His bare feet scuffed against the scatter rugs as he limped into the dining room. "Mr. Wilkes," he said with a certain sarcasm, "won't you join me in a taste?"

"Oh, Papa!" Salena protested.

Carlton stepped between her and her father and pulled the flask from his jacket. "I owe you one, Mr. Parrish."

"I suppose you do." Mr. Parrish took a shot glass from the sideboard and held it for Carlton to fill.

"Papa," Salena said, "Carlton was just leaving."

Motioning to the sofa, Mr. Parrish invited Carlton to sit. "I'm sure he got more gumption than to come into a man's house in the middle of the night, wake him up and then *leave.* Besides, this Paris thing got me so I can't sleep." He sat. "Carlton, I'm a country man and I didn't have the privilege of the education that yo' daddy give you. But I do my share of readin' and I read about these colored fellows that run off to Paris cause they can't be free in this country. But you take a look at what they do, and they all singers and horn players. That's their *work.* I understand that some of them make good money at it, too." He sipped the liquor. "Now you see what I'm gettin' at? I don't hear you or Salena singin' or playing no horn. Lord, the girl's momma couldn't even get her to sing in the church choir. So tell me what you gone do in Paris? You just be livin' off what yo' daddy left you—givin' it all away to another bunch of white men. Now, I know things are supposed to be better overseas, but let me tell you this. No matter how bad it gets, and it done already been a hell of a lot worse than it is now, there is no place like your home." Finishing his drink, he started back up the stairs, then stopped and looked plainly at Carlton and shook his head. "You know, Carlton, Salena my only child."

The old man went up into the darkness, and Carlton turned to Salena. "I could look into getting passports tomorrow."

Salena threw her head back and sighed. "Carlton…I love you, but really…it's a silly idea."

▼ ▼ ▼

The sun was above the rooftops when Mr. Shannon rapped on the window of Carlton's Lincoln. "I just wanted to see if you were all right, Mr. Wilkes."

Carlton's head was cloudy, and his neck ached from having slept on the armrest. He mumbled a greeting to Mr. Shannon and felt in his pocket for the keys. "Excuse me, I must have fallen asleep..."

"Don't worry about it." Mr. Shannon winked. "I remember when my wife and I were courting—besides, it's good to be young. Why don't you come in and have a cup of coffee and some eggs? Put something solid in your stomach."

Carlton tried to beg off the invitation, but Mr. Shannon insisted, and he found himself brushing the wrinkles out of his suit and running his tongue over his stale teeth.

Inside Mrs. Shannon, her hair in rollers, was scrambling eggs. She was a tall, dark woman with genteel features. Two girls sat at the kitchen table, one the little girl Carlton had seen the day before and the other an adolescent who seemed much perturbed by his appearance.

"I'll just have coffee."

"Oh, no, you won't," said Mrs. Shannon as she scooped grits and soft scrambled eggs onto a plate with sausage patties, toast and jam. The food smelled good and Carlton was hungry; he fidgeted to prevent himself from eating until all were seated and Mr. Shannon had said the grace. The older girl, Gloria, pretended to ignore him. She ate the sausages with her fingers, pinky up. Mrs. Shannon firmly told her to use a fork, and slowly, fastidiously wiping grease from her fingers onto a paper napkin, Gloria conformed. The little girl hardly ate for staring at him. He winked at her, trying to solicit a smile, and asked her name. She turned away, but prodded by her parents she told him, "Bonita."

"That's a pretty name. Spanish, isn't it?"

"I believe so," Mrs. Shannon said. "We took it from her grandmother."

Mrs. Shannon asked about the wedding plans. "Salena tells me nothing, you know. Not that it's my business, but a neighbor would like to know."

"We haven't set them yet," Carlton said. "Maybe soon. We've been thinking about going to Europe."

"That would be a nice honeymoon." Mrs. Shannon looked impressed. "I swear, Salena doesn't tell me a thing."

"She hasn't exactly agreed yet," Carlton confessed.

"It is expensive," Mrs. Shannon said slowly. For a moment it seemed to Carlton that she would give him a sympathetic pat on the hand. "You'd better travel while you are young. Once you have your children you'll be settled for a long time."

"I did get to travel over in the Pacific during the war, or 'the conflict'—whatever they called it. Korea." Mr. Shannon piped in between bites of egg and toast. He stopped chewing and looked at Carlton. "What you think about all this mess that Shuttlesworth and King stirred up, Mr. Wilkes? You think it gonna come to something?"

This was not the conversation Carlton wanted. He wanted to ignore Mr. Shannon and to turn back to Bonita with her erect braids and tiny, square, egg-covered teeth.

"We don't need to talk about that at the table," Mrs. Shannon said. And then more softly, "It upsets the children."

"Some children are out there in jail."

Mrs. Shannon scooted back from the table, asked if Carlton wanted a second helping, and barely waiting for him to clear his mouth to reply, she put another spoonful of grits on his plate.

"Some children are in jail," Mr. Shannon repeated. "I can't say that I'm not scared for them, but there comes a time when you got to—"

"Got to do nothing." Mrs. Shannon banged the pot on the stove. "None of mine are going down there to be killed by Bull Connor."

"I'm not scared of Bull Connor," the older girl said.

"You'd better be," her mother replied. She took a breath. "We're going to upset Bonita, so just let it rest."

"It won't rest." Mr. Shannon took his plate to the sink. "Mr. Wilkes,

I'm going downtown. I think a lot of us will be marching."

Mrs. Shannon cut a look at him. "You'd better be marching on to work, instead of jail. We don't have any money to get you out."

"Then I'll just stay." He went to the door. "Are you coming, Mr. Wilkes?"

Slowly, Carlton sat back from the table. He nodded toward Mrs. Shannon and stood. He felt a tremble in his knee. Gloria popped up and ran toward her father. "Can I go with you?" she asked.

▼ ▼ ▼

The park was crowded with people of all ages. Carlton recognized no one, but Mr. Shannon, a schoolteacher, greeted many of the people, both adults and children. Policemen and firemen were gathering on three sides of them. Yet there was quiet festivity, as people greeted friends or sang hymns. Someone was singing *Gonna lay down my burden, down by the riverside...*Someone else led a small group in prayer.

A bullhorn crackled, and the crowd began to shift. Carlton's mind tripped over itself as he tried to fathom everything. He couldn't understand the instructions coming from the demonstration leaders. The bullhorn seemed to be circling the park. He thought it might be coming from Bull Connor's armored car, yet he couldn't see the car. He looked for Mr. Shannon and saw the top of his curly head several yards away. He tried to follow, but the crowd pressed against him and Mr. Shannon moved even further away. It occurred to him that the people were dressed nicely, in clean dungarees and sundresses, and that the firemen were preparing to hose them as they had done to the children the day before.

Behind the fire trucks and paddy wagons he saw Uncle Booker's insurance building. He thought that if he could make it past the trucks, he might be able to take refuge in the building. What Mr. Parrish had said was evident now. How much business would the store owners along Fourth Avenue do if there were rioting in the park? They had mortgages to pay and families to feed.

The demonstrators, singing and chanting, lined up at the park's edge. Carlton was close enough to see the face of one of the firemen. He was a square-jawed young man, covered with freckles. He held the hose against his body with one arm and gripped the throat of the nozzle with his hand.

Suddenly Bull Connor's armored car rolled down the street between the crowd and the firemen. At the window sat heavy-jowled Bull Connor himself. He wiped his glasses with a white hankie and spoke into a microphone which was amplified by a speaker on the roof of the car. The demonstrators did not disband, and the car moved on. A line of helmeted policemen and their dogs moved in, cutting off Carlton's retreat to Uncle Booker's building.

The young fireman adjusted the nozzle. It seemed to have been pointed directly at Carlton, but there was some confusion. The fireman was looking back at the pumper and yelling instructions. The men at the pumper had taken out their wrenches and were tampering with the hydrant intakes. The young fireman took aim again and braced himself. Carlton saw him push down the nozzle lever.

There was still an escape route, Carlton thought, if he could get to the back of the crowd and then slip behind the fire trucks. He began to push through the crowd. Things were getting too crazy. Somebody was bound to get hurt. Negro progress was supposed to be good for Negroes; he was a Negro, but this was not good for him. He would go to Europe. He pushed faster through the crowd, not caring whom he shoved or stepped on. If Salena didn't want to go, he would go without her. Someone grabbed his shoulder. He pulled away and was grabbed again. It was Mr. Shannon. "Hold on a minute, Mr. Wilkes. We are marching on City Hall."

Carlton was still for a moment. Mr. Shannon's hand felt like a vise on his shoulder. Then he shivered, and Mr. Shannon took away his hand.

"I'm sorry," Mr. Shannon said and looked away. Carlton flushed with embarrassment. Mr. Shannon spoke again, in a steady low voice. "Won't you please walk with me, Mr. Wilkes? If you won't, I'm not sure that I can."

For awhile, Carlton could not answer, and the two men stood while the crowd pushed around them. "Mr. Shannon," Carlton's voice quavered, "I'm afraid." The confession was accompanied with a great relief, but relief made him no less afraid.

"I'm afraid, too." Mr. Shannon hooked his arm in Carlton's and slowly the two got in step with the crowd. "But I feel I don't have much choice about being here. I've got my children to think about, for one thing. You're young, Mr. Wilkes. You don't have children yet, but someday you will. When you have children, then you will know that you have to make a choice to face your fears. I don't know what will happen today. We may be knocked in the head, maybe worse. Just keep thinking about the children. Think about all the children."

"All the children?"

"The children who were arrested."

Carlton tried to imagine the faces of the children. He imagined groups of children, their faces blurred by distance. He saw them as silhouettes or as flashes of color dashing in and out of the arcs of water. He saw the form of the boy who had been knocked down by the water. But he could not see the children as individuals, as people he knew. Because his father had money, he had been sent away to a boarding school in the North. Except for business, he had had only a little contact with these people, much less with their children. It had been a business errand to the hospital that had brought him and Salena together.

"Salena," he thought out loud. He had no children, but he had a future with Salena. He tried to imagine having children with Salena. How would they look? Her eyes? His nose? Her mouth and hair? Try as he might, he couldn't imagine the child's face.

▼ ▼ ▼

Two by two, the demonstrators began to file across the street toward a gap between the police cars and the fire trucks. Secure on Mr. Shannon's arm, Carlton fell into step. They made it to where the park lawn and the pavement met before the line stopped. The demonstration leaders argued with the policemen. Again, Carlton saw the young, freckled fireman, now dragging the dead weight of his limp hose around and aiming it at the marchers. There was a murmur, and people began to kneel. Kneeling! Carlton thought. Kneeling like lambs to be slaughtered. He tried to pull away.

"Kneel and pray," someone said. "Kneel and pray."

Mr. Shannon held him tightly. "They say pray that the water won't come on, Mr. Wilkes."

Carlton shook his head.

"They are praying that the water won't come on."

They had gone crazy. It was one thing to get hosed when you were on your feet and able to run, but it was suicide to kneel down. Mr. Shannon pulled on him, his knees buckled and he landed squarely on the edge of the sidewalk.

The water didn't come.

"Oh, God. Oh, God."

People sang and prayed. Carlton dared not move. It was as if the collective will of the crowd had frozen the hydrants. If he could only stay here now. Stay. If he didn't move. If he didn't shiver. If he were as still as ice, then the water wouldn't come. Time would hold still. He caught his breath. His ears began to ring. But nothing, nothing moved. Except now, a cold molecule of sweat was slowly pushing through a pore at the base of his scalp, and swelling into a quivering bead. He must not move! "Oh, God, oh, God." He imagined the boy, rolled in the streets by the jets of white water, and the dogs—oh God, the dogs. Why was he a Negro and so scared?

The eyes of the young fireman were round, and the hose had slipped from under his arm. He was backing away from the crowd, looking over his shoulder to his colleagues for support.

Carlton saw the fireman stepping back. It confused him. His concentration slipped and he began to note his surroundings. He was kneeling in a crowd, being held by a man he barely knew, while the firemen backed away and tampered with the hydrants. He had stepped out of his life into something stranger than life. He had a comfortable home which sat on a hill above Titusville. He had a fianceé who was one of the first colored nurses at the white hospital. He had a business to run and a Lincoln Continental.

Yet he was compelled to stay where he was, on his knees, in front of Bull Connor's firemen. For if he moved, if one hair sprung up from the pomade that held it close to his skull, then the water would come on. The bead of sweat trembled and began to roll in a meandering, ticklish path over his temple and across his cheek. That wasn't his fault! He couldn't help that. He hadn't done anything to cause it to fall.

Now other beads began to roll. He felt each one individually as it prickled across his skin. Each one was a cold prod inciting his body to revolt, to shiver, to stand up and run. But if he dared, then it would be the end of him. He would be rolled in the streets, chased and bitten by the dogs. He would be no better than the others.

"Courage, Mr. Wilkes. Courage." Mr. Shannon loosened his grip, and Carlton screamed and jerked away.

"Kneel, mister," someone said, but Carlton continued stumbling through the kneeling people, stepping on them, picking a route to the rear of the park.

Then there was a whoosh. Carlton turned to see the young fireman brace himself as the hose kicked and foamed and shot water. At first the stream scoured the asphalt and sprayed up a milky, prismatic mist; then the fireman gained control of it and directed it at the kneeling demonstrators.

The jets bowled the demonstrators over and knocked them down as they tried to rise. White arcs came from every direction, and Carlton realized that he was surrounded. He pushed people aside as he ran instinctively toward Uncle Booker's building. He made it to the curb just as a column of water came at him. Diving behind a parked car, he escaped the direct force. He edged along the side of the car and peeped around the fender to see in which direction the hose was pointed.

Just inside the park, he saw a young woman in a white dress. She was bent over and stumbling as she tried to dodge the jets of water. Carlton wiped his eyes to get a better look. His heart skipped a beat. Was it Salena? He wiped his eyes again. The young woman turned in his direction, and he saw that without a doubt it was Salena. Now she had stopped running and was trying to help a heavyset man out of the mud.

Carlton ducked behind the car again. His head was spinning and the water in his eyes had broken the world into fragments. He had a clear shot to Uncle Booker's building. If he tried to reach Salena the hoses would surely catch him. He tried to convince himself that she would be all right. She was strong, stronger than himself. Maybe she was too strong for him. Maybe he couldn't imagine children with her because they had no future together. She was claiming her future, here at the park. His future was in Europe.

He tried to imagine Salena's face. He held it in his mind for a moment, but it seemed the water in his eyes was also in his head. Every time he got the image of her to stand still, it was washed away by rivulets of water. Maybe he didn't love her. If he loved her, then he would be able to see her clearly. He would be able to run to her.

He looked for her again in the crowd and in a moment found her. The white uniform was now gray with mud. She had lost her shoes. She seemed dazed, no longer crouched and running but standing and limping, an easy target. Then he saw a jet of water coming toward her. "Salena!" He stood. The scene kept spinning around him. First Uncle Booker's building, then Salena, then the fire trucks. "Run," he heard someone scream at him. "Run, run, run!" It was himself screaming. He ran. He wasn't sure in what direction. The water punched his ribs and knocked out his breath. It slammed him to the asphalt, shoved his hips against the pavement and beat on his back. He lay and caught his breath as the runoff trickled and fizzed around him. Slowly he stood and made a clumsy step toward Salena.

# Hollow and Far Away

▼
▼
▼

I laughed when my son asked if I had ever seen a flying saucer. I was sitting in my big chair in the den when he came to me with eyes so round and teary that I rubbed my hand across his bristled hair and drew him close. I told him there was no such thing—it was just a figment of somebody's imagination. But I remember a time, back in the sixties, though I can't say for sure whether it was a dream or not, that I watched a light chasing our car as we sped down a crackling gravel road through the woods. The light trailed just off the right side of the car, like the full moon, appearing and disappearing behind the trees, a glow gently alternating from white to red.

I remember (though I could have dreamed it) my mother's almond-shaped eyes widening and her slow, strained voice coming from the front seat, "Roll up the window, Ralphie, roll up the window. Be a good boy, and roll up the window." Poor Josie, my sister, just four, sat in Momma's lap and pushed her finger against the pane. She giggled. Momma pulled her finger away from the window and Josie put it back. "Roll up the window, Ralphie, please, be a good boy, and roll up the window." I remember nothing my father said, only that he gripped the steering wheel so tightly his knuckles looked like stones.

Slowly I screwed up the window, closing off the wet breeze, heavy with honeysuckle, closing off the delightful, musical silence the light made in the woods. Daddy won't whip us tonight, I thought, Daddy won't whip us tonight.

▼ ▼ ▼

Earlier, we had eaten supper with Daddy's aunt and uncle, Sadie and Ralph. Country people didn't give out formal invitations that often; supper was reserved for holidays or for preachers, but Aunt and Uncle had lived in New Jersey for twenty-five years and had picked up city customs. Childless, they had retired to the country and, having little to do with their money, spent it on a big house and a big car, or at least big to us. Uncle Ralph was always saying how Daddy was his favorite nephew and the only one in our family besides himself who was trying to make something of himself. "Discipline is half the battle," Uncle always said. "Discipline and opportunity."

Momma had dressed us up and Daddy had warned us to be on our damned best behavior. Aunt had the table set up with candies and glass bowls and two forks and plates for bread. Even though Momma said she thought we ought to drink out of plastic cups, Aunt waved her off and said, "Surely they mature enough to drink out of a glass." I felt proud that Aunt had called me "mature." It wasn't the same as saying I was "big" or "old enough." "Mature" was one of those words, like "discipline," that seemed to bestow on us an important responsibility.

Uncle sat in an armchair at the head of the table and poured real wine for Momma and Daddy. I could tell Momma was uncomfortable with this finery, but I was enjoying it. I had seen tables set this way on *As the World Turns* and *The Guiding Light.* Uncle slapped Daddy on the shoulder and reared back in his chair. "You see, white people ain't the only ones who know how to set a table." He asked me if I wanted some wine; when I said I did, he bellowed.

"Ought not tease the boy," Aunt fussed. "Don't need no drinking habit at his age."

Uncle splashed a little wine in my glass, saying, "Taste won't hurt nobody. 'Sides, them white people over in Italy let their children drink all the wine they want. Wine with every meal. Give it to the babies. Yes, sir, I saw that in '44."

Aunt passed the bowls around and told Momma to help herself. Then she slipped one out the side of her mouth, "This here ain't no It'ly."

I looked at Daddy to see whether or not I was supposed to drink the wine or whether it was a joke. Daddy wasn't giving me a clue. He was looking at Momma serving Josie's plate, and I could see beads of sweat on his clean-shaven lip. When Uncle put his napkin in his lap, Daddy waited a minute, then pulled his own off his plate and placed it in his lap. "Put your napkin on your knee, son," he said. I had never seen cloth napkins and thought they were tea towels.

"Oh, no," cried Aunt. "Surely, he's too young to put a napkin on his lap." She came around the table and tied the napkin around my neck. "See, this is what a sweet, young boy does, so he don't spill food on his clothes."

Daddy grinned, almost laughed, and shook his head a little. "He bet' not spill no food." Until that moment, I hadn't worried about spilling food, but with Daddy acting nervous, I began to feel nervous, too.

"Big boy like dat," Uncle said. "He ain't gone waste hard-earned food when some people just down the road going hungry. Now, I done seen some hungry people—white and colored. Come right down to it though, they don't know how to control their resources. They have this great bunch of children and know they can't feed 'em. Now you tell me, if a man know he just making seventy-five or a hundred dollars a week and got to pay off his house and car, what he doing having all them mouths he can't feed? That's what keeps our people poor. White man, least the *smart* white man, you don't see him with no more than two—three children."

"Two is a nice number," Aunt said. "One of each."

After Uncle mumbled a quick prayer, Momma sipped her wine and said it tasted like the champagne that she and Daddy had at their wedding. Uncle said that he had good champagne when he lived in Jersey up near Union and that you couldn't get good champagne down here.

Momma smiled, and it gave me a good feeling. Her lips were full and painted red. When she smiled her eyes crinkled at the edges, and her head tilted a little, causing her hair to fall a little over her forehead. She looked like a movie star to me. "It sure was good to me," she said firmly.

"That's because you don't know nothing," Daddy said, like he was kicking her under the table. Momma stopped smiling and didn't eat for a moment either.

I took a sip of the wine. It was very sweet and I liked it.

"What you doing, Ralphie?" Daddy asked me keenly. "Couldn't you see Uncle just teasing you?"

Uncle slapped the tabletop with his palm and laughed. "That little bit ain't gone hurt 'im. Make him a man."

"No such thing," Aunt said and took my glass and set it between her and Josie. "Liable to stunt his growth. Besides, Bob don't want his children growing up to be no alcoholics. Parents need to set straight by they children."

"Now that's what I say, too," Uncle said. "Discipline and opportunity. But a little wine ain't gone kill 'im."

Then Josie squealed. She had tried to lift her glass and tipped over my glass that Aunt had put next to her. The wine spread out in a pink stain on the white tablecloth. Momma went into a fit of apologies and tried to wipe up the pool with her napkin, and then realized she was ruining the napkin, too. Aunt ran for a rag and kept telling Momma that a little bleach would get it right out, all she had to do was to soak it overnight. Uncle Ralph let out a bray and said he would just buy another one. It wasn't nothing but a tablecloth, and the little girl don't know no better.

During all the fussing Daddy was quiet and stiff. He wasn't chewing but his jaw was working like he was grinding his teeth. I felt sorry for Josie. She just looked around shyly and held her lips firm, because crying in this case wouldn't do any good.

▼ ▼ ▼

After supper we all went into the den. I felt special in the den, because it was like a children's living room, and the closest we had to it was a dining room where we did our homework. Uncle had a La-Z-Boy, and Aunt had a stuffed chair with a little ottoman. The walls were made of pine panels with big brown knots. "Knotty pine," Momma called it. She would sigh when she said it, and I knew how badly she wanted a house like this, with knotty pine and tile and wall-to-wall carpeting in the bedrooms and, most of all, brick on the outside. But not even Uncle and Aunt had red brick. Uncle said he didn't want it. He didn't want to advertise to the Ku Klux Klan what he had.

Momma kept offering to help wash the dishes, but Aunt said no, that she would get them after *Ed Sullivan,* and to go ahead and make herself comfortable on the couch. We children sat on the floor, but Daddy kept staring down at us to make sure we were sitting straight and not rolling around in our good clothes.

I felt a prickling on the back of my head, like a ghost hand was bristling up my hair. This is the way Daddy made me feel when he got in that quiet, tense mood where he wanted everything to go right, and nothing would. He had been that way off and on for a good while because things weren't going right at work.

Daddy was the only black man on his job. He was a good refrigeration mechanic, having gone for training in Baltimore, and he was union. Only one of the white men who worked with him, a minister, was anywhere near friendly. He was the only one who would eat with Daddy, and once he refused to sit inside a restaurant with the rest of the men because the restaurant wouldn't let Daddy in. Daddy had to go around to a cubbyhole in the back to order his lunch, and eat it outside. Hearing about it was enough to make me want to hate all white people, but I couldn't—I didn't—because of this one nice man. I had to keep reminding myself that for every five or six bad ones, there was one nice one, and you couldn't always assume which one was the nice one.

But that nice man had left, and now Daddy had no one between him and the others. Every evening when he came home he looked a little shaken. Momma would look worried, and she would whisper that he should quit. But he would say, it is such an opportunity. Such an opportunity. He would drink and ask to see schoolwork and things would get worse.

First *Lassie* came on, and we could barely hear it for all the grown-up noise, especially Uncle talking about politics, most of which didn't make sense to me. He would skip around a lot, talking about ole Eisenhower and then about ole Johnson and what he got no business doing over there starting another Korea. Then he would say something about the Red Russians and the Red Chinese and how you couldn't trust them, and the next thing you know we going to have all them foreign countries flying red flags.

"But at least the Red Russians ain't killing no colored folks," Aunt said. She whined when she argued politics with Uncle. She would let him go for awhile, booming out his opinions, and then slip in a comment here and there. They sounded like a duet of boom and whine. "And every man and woman in Russia got a good job, too. They say half the women are doctors."

"A woman doctor!" Uncle shook his head. "They just made 'em doctors. You got to work to make yo'self a doctor. Don't mean you good at something just 'cause you got the title." He paused a moment, but before Aunt could slip in he said, "Bob know what I'm talkin' about. Don't you, Bob?"

Daddy didn't say anything but sat square on the sofa beside Momma and slowly rubbed his hands together.

"Maybe we could use a highball," Aunt said.

"Please no," Momma said, slipping toward the edge of the couch to catch Aunt. But she was too late.

Uncle Ralph was talking about how a colored man had to work twice as hard and be twice as smart. Aunt set down a tray with bottles and glasses of ice and fixed drinks for the grown-ups.

"They tell me little Ralph is the smartest one in his class. Even in the white school," she said. That year our county had gone to the Freedom of Choice, and lucky for me Daddy had freely chosen to send me to the white school. Aunt handed a highball to Momma, and when Momma didn't take it, Daddy took it and handed it to her.

I was the only black boy in the fifth grade, and the teacher was hard and didn't like me. But Daddy was even harder than the teacher. Every Sunday I had to show him my graded schoolwork, and he would give me a whack for every problem I missed. Daddy was no easy whacker, and no matter how much effort I put into it, I was no good at math. "Your job is easy," he would say after he had punished me. "All you have to do is bring good grades home. Wait until you get out into the world, then you'll see what I have to go through." The other black fifth-grader was a girl, my only friend. At recess, when the other children romped, she helped me with my math.

Even before we were halfway through *Lassie* Josie started to roll on the floor, and Daddy said, half under his breath, for me to keep an eye on her. He had a way of talking to me so that I heard him plain like he was speaking in a normal voice, but people around us (except for Momma) didn't hear it. It seemed the quieter he whispered, the keener my ears got. I pulled Josie onto my lap and tried to make her pay attention to the television.

"A Negro's got to pull hisself up by his own bootstraps," Uncle exclaimed, "and if he ain't got boots, then he just better walk barefoot 'til he gets a pair." He bellowed. Aunt harrumphed. Daddy let out a wooden chuckle that kind of came up and hit me in the back of the head. I sat stiff and held Josie between my knees, and hoped that chuckle would come again, this time softer. Instead I heard ice clinking in his glass.

"Can I get you another one, Bob?" Aunt said.

I looked at Momma, sitting beside Daddy, her feet placed together, her hands holding her glass on her lap. She faced straight ahead, her lips tight and her eyes closed.

Daddy cleared his throat. "I b'leve I will."

Just then Josie broke my hold and rolled off my legs. On the screen, Timmy lay unconscious and Lassie was licking his face to bring him around. For a little while I had a dog, a beagle I named Lightning. But Daddy took Lightning away from me, said I was spoiling him for hunting. One day, deep in the winter, Lightning ran away. We followed his tracks through the snow for miles until suddenly they stopped as if Lightning had sprouted wings and flown off. Daddy stared for a long time at where the tracks stopped, while the woods got gloomy and the sunset looked like a fringe of fire around the ice-laden world. Daddy said if he ever caught up with that damn dog he would shoot him.

Josie went up and put a handprint on the screen. Daddy cried out and startled her, but she didn't cry. She ran to Momma. Uncle and Aunt laughed and said that it was all right. Aunt said that a little Windex was all you needed to get a handprint off the TV screen, and then Uncle said you couldn't spray it while it was hot because it might explode, and then Aunt said, no such thing and that she had better sense anyway than to spray a hot TV.

Then the show the adults had been waiting for came on, and I started to wish we were at home watching it so it would be quieter and we could be in our regular clothes. There were a number of acts, including a woman with a lamb puppet that I thought was OK, and some circus people, a comedian and some white people singing. Then came the act they had been waiting for, and they all got quiet. It was the colored act. That night it was James Brown, whom they had never heard of, and they were very disappointed that it wasn't Nat King Cole or Duke Ellington.

"Who that boy?" Uncle asked. Aunt said she didn't know, that she couldn't hear because he was running his mouth so much, and then he looked at Daddy and Daddy asked me if I had heard it sitting up to the TV as close as I was. I hadn't heard it, but I knew who he was from school, so I said it was James Brown and that he was a soul singer.

"Where you learn that?" Daddy asked. "What you mean a 'soul singer'?"

I knew because my girlfriend from school had told me. Besides teaching me math, she kept me current on the latest music. She had learned it from her cousins in D.C. who owned all the new records; her parents, like mine, would never have allowed a James Brown record in the house.

"Religious?" Aunt Sadie asked. "Soul like gospel?" Then she shook her head. "He ain't gospel, shaking his hips like that."

Uncle Ralph brayed, and Daddy spoke to me again, except quiet now like his voice was a sharp little penknife. "You know he ain't no soul singer."

"Soul don't mean religious," I said, and I could see Daddy was getting red. Momma patted his knee which was rocking a little, I could feel the vibration of his heel tapping, tapping against the wood floor. But I knew I was right, and I hadn't done nothing, so I just followed Momma's cue which was to turn around and watch TV and to hope he would forget about it.

James Brown was sweating and crying and down on his knees, and a man came from back of the stage and put a cape around him. He was saying, "Please don't go, please don't go," and the man started to take him off the stage.

"Isn't that shameful," Aunt said. "Come up and make a monkey of hisself like that on TV. Did you ever see such a thing? Most colored people doing all we can so they won't call us monkeys."

James Brown threw off the cape and came back to the microphone and cried and danced some more. Uncle Ralph bellowed and Aunt said James Brown was trying to take over the *Ed Sullivan Show.* "They will never let him back on the show again. And it's a good thing, too."

The man put the cape on James Brown again and started to lead him away, but James Brown threw it off and came back to the microphone. "Lawd have mercy," Aunt said.

Her mouth was open and her palm was pressed against her cheek. Even Uncle was quiet, just gaping at James Brown. I looked at Momma and Josie. Momma was holding her hands over Josie's ears and had her eyes closed. Daddy was looking at me.

I knew what was going to happen now and there was nothing I could do about it. I could try to be good, and just *maybe* he would cool down before we got home. But it didn't matter one bit; if he wanted to whip, he would whip, no matter what time of night or day. It didn't matter if I pretended to be asleep or how much Momma begged him not to; if he wanted to whip, he would.

"Why don't he just get off the stage?" Aunt said. "That's just what they think of colored folks, just take over."

"Nawh, nawh," Uncle said, "that's part of the act. Do you reckon that's part of the act?"

"Whoever heard of an act like that! Acting like a fool, that's all."

"Nawh. He making money. He givin' the people what they want—some excitement. You reckon that a part of the act, little Ralph?"

I heard the question plain enough and had an opinion, too, but I looked at Daddy. Daddy's temples throbbed and his eyes were glazed. "Didn't you hear Uncle Ralph speak to you?" His voice was keen. I turned to answer Uncle, but he cut me off asking the question again, and I wasn't supposed to interrupt a grown-up.

"Yes, sir. Yes, sir." I said. "It's part of the act. He is taking the opportunity to put on."

"No such a thing," Aunt said. "He just acting a fool. It's shameful you can't let colored folks do nothing less they act their color."

"The boy said it part of the act."

"What does he know about this foolishness, as little as he is? You don't know about this foolishness, do you, little Ralph?"

"No, ma'am."

"I didn't think he was one of those kind of little boys. Bob raise' his children too good to have them listening to that kind of monkey business."

"He know, too," Uncle Ralph said and clucked his tongue. "He said he know, he know."

▼ ▼ ▼

Daddy had started the car and waited while Uncle, holding the door handle, had his last say about things. I lay my chin in the open window. The air was chilly for late summer. The stars were icy glints hanging over the fields. The belt of the Milky Way cut the sky in half.

For some reason, I thought about Lightning. It may have been the sudden crispness in the air, or the stars. I remembered that as we left the woods the evening we tracked him, I kept thinking I heard him. The snow was getting crusty, so it could have been the crunch of the ice beneath our boots. With each step, I thought I heard a faraway yip, yip, yip calling to me. I stopped to listen better and Daddy hollered at me to hurry up.

As we pulled away from Aunt and Uncle's to begin our hour's drive home, I saw two pinpoints of red moving along the horizon. So slowly they moved that at first I thought they were stars, red stars. I didn't think they were Martians, though I may have hoped they were. When we were driving between the fields, the sky was big and the lights far away. I wasn't afraid. I may have fallen asleep.

I remember we were on the dirt road, speeding through the woods, and Momma's strained voice was telling me to roll up the window. We came to a bottom where there was a glow, red and orange, and Daddy stopped the car. A light from behind caught up to us. It was a police light going around and around, reflecting off the slick bark of the trees along the creek bottom. In the woods, we saw white forms, floating like ghosts, over the banks and alighting in the road. "Lock the door, Ralphie," Momma said through her teeth. Daddy started to open his door and Momma's look cut him off.

The figures surrounded the car. There may have been six. The police light turned their robes red and white and their conical shadows fell across the trunk and the rear window. One of them shook the car and pushed its spook face against the rear window. I moved to the middle of the backseat and squeezed down near the axle hump.

Another tapped on Daddy's window, and Momma said,

"Don't roll it down." Her words moved like a rustle in the trees. Daddy rolled the window down halfway.

"Yes, suh," Daddy said. His voice was steady but distorted with tension. A flashlight shone on his face and silhouetted the back of his round head and long neck.

"That ain't him," one of them said. They were all around us, peering at us through the squares cut into their hoods.

"Is too him. Look like the car."

"Whar you coming from, boy?"

"I been up to my uncle's house," Daddy said.

"You out mighty late to be visiting when you got to be working tomorrow."

"My aunt, she right sick."

"Mighty dressed up to be visitin'. You wouldn't've been up to no nigger meeting, would cha?"

"Just teach 'em a lesson anyway. Don't matter which one." One of them shook the car and it rocked like a boat.

"No, suh, been up to see my aunt."

The flashlight shone on each of us. Momma's eyes were like shiny black buttons, a look I have seen on birds when I ventured too close to their nests. Josie's face was frozen, just short of combusting into crying. "Ain't she a cute little thing?"

Then the light cast its cold tranquillity on me. The bright teardrop bulb and its flickering blue filament fixed me. All the world seemed white and frozen, and a faraway voice came to me.

"What's yo' aunt's name, boy?"

Daddy started to answer, and the voice cut him off.

"I'm talking to the *li'l* boy. What's yo' aunt's name?"

"Go 'head 'n' get 'im," said another voice.

"We want to get the riidt one. What's yo' aunt's name, li'l boy?"

The light moved out of my eyes. For a moment I saw globules of color, oranges and yellows, and an intrusion of black silhouettes, the back of my father's head, the white face with the eyes cut out.

"She, Aunt Sadie," I said.

"Aunt Sadie." The voice was nearly tender. "She sick? What she got?"

"The gall bladder, I think."

"Who care what she got?" another voice said. "Tell me this, boy. You go to school?"

"Yes, suh."

"Whar at?"

I knew what to answer. "Colored school."

"Now don't lie to me. You know what happen to nigger boys that lie. We cut off yo' balls and make yo' momma eat 'em." He laughed.

I shrank behind the seat; the light found me.

"Ain't that right?" The light went to Daddy. *"Ain't that right?"*

"Dat's right," Daddy said slowly.

"Ain't it *funny?* Eat yo' balls?"

"Yeah, it funny."

"You don't sound like you think it funny. Laugh."

"I think it's funny, suh."

"Laugh, then."

Daddy tried to laugh. At first he coughed, then his throat whistled. The man threw back his head, almost losing his hood, he laughed so hard. The others joined him, one banging his palms on the trunk of the car, another lying against the windows and leaning on the roof to support himself.

Then the light came back to me. "Whar yo' daddy work, boy?"

I couldn't think of what to say. "Whar he work?"

Then I thought. "The sawmill."

"You wouldn't be lying?"

"No, sir."

"What you say?"

"No, suh."

"You sure dat's what you say? You di'n't say nothin' uppity, did you?"

"No, suh."

"I di'n't think so." The light went back on Daddy. "So yo' daddy work at the sawmill with all the other niggers, ain't that riidt? He wouldn't be one of them uppity niggers work over at the plant. He wouldn't be no union nigger cause if he was he find hisself chained upside a tree. Ain't that riidt?" And then, hollow and far away, "You love yo' daddy, boy?"

"Niggers don't love," another voice said.

"Sure they do, leastwise this boy does. You love yo' daddy, boy?"

I opened my mouth, but my throat had closed off.

"I ain't hear that. What you say, boy?"

"Leave 'em 'lone," another voice said.

"You love 'im, you see to it he don't cause no trouble." He kicked at the car. Daddy put the car into gear; it stalled. He cranked it, got it into gear and slowly we rolled down the crackling road to the bottom, across the creaking bridge, and up the hill, out of the woods, into the starlit fields.

That night we weren't whipped. The next day my father went to work at the sawmill. I did not return to the white school until the government forced integration three years later. Whenever we saw a mysterious light or sometimes mistook a ripe moon playing hide-and-seek with the trees for something else, we said nothing, nothing at all, about it.

# Food That Pleases, Food to Take Home

▼
▼
▼

Annie McPhee wasn't sure about what Mary Taliferro was telling her. Mary said that colored people in Louisa should stand up for their rights. They were doing it in the cities. Mary said that Channel Six from Richmond had shown pictures of Negroes sitting in at lunch counters. She laughed that "colored people" were becoming "Negroes." Walter Cronkite had shown pictures from Albany and Birmingham. Negroes were on the move.

On the church lawn one bright Sunday, Mary caught hold of Annie's arm and whispered, "What choo think of Reverend Green's sermon?" She knew Annie had eyes for Reverend Green.

"It was nice," Annie said. She pushed the pillbox back onto her head and patted her flip curl.

"But don't you think he was right about doing something?"

" 'Course he right," Annie said with a smack of her lips, "but ain't nobody gone do nothing." Then she saw a glint in Mary's eye. "What you gone do and where?"

"We could march."

"Who gone march?" Mary held her hat against the wind that rustled through the fallen oak leaves.

"We could organize a march downtown. We could march down Main Street and tell them white folks that we want our rights."

"And that'll be the end of it, girl. Who gone march with you? Everybody around here is scared to march."

Mary pulled on Annie's elbow and guided her away from the folks gathering in front of the clapboard church to the pebbly space next to the cemetery. "I know what you thinking, girl. But I'm too tired of it to be scared. I wish something *would* happen around here and I figure we just the ones to start it."

"*You* the one." Annie put on her dark glasses. "Tell me who I look like?"

"Hummph." Mary turned up her lips for a second. "I don't know, girl. Elizabeth Taylor?"

"Nurrrh, child. You know I don't look like no 'Lizabeth Taylor. Somebody else. Somebody even more famous than that."

"Richard Burton."

"I'm gone kill you. Do I look like a man?" Annie gave Mary one more chance: she stepped back, her heel sinking into the soft hill of a grave, and put her hands on her hips. The wind folded her dress against her thighs. "Look at the hair and the glasses."

Mary frowned as she examined Annie and finally she gave up.

"Jackie Kennedy! Don't I look just like Jackie Kennedy?"

"Yeah, with the sunglasses, I guess you do," Mary said. "Anybody would, even me, if I had them sunglasses on."

"It'll take more than a pair of sunglasses..."

"But for real," Mary continued and started toward the parking lot, "we could start something. We could make the news if we did something in Louisa. I can just see myself sittin' up there on Walter Cronkite."

"Sittin' in the Louisa jail be more like it. Them white folks don't want no trouble."

"It don't matter what *they* want. Just like Reverend Green said, it matter what's right."

"Then how come *he* ain't doing it?"

"I bet he will if somebody started it. You know he's a preacher and he just can't run out and start no stuff." Mary placed her palms on the hood of the used Fairlane she had bought in Richmond with a down payment she had saved from factory work. She leaned up on her toes as Reverend Green was known to do and deepened her voice. "The Lord helps them that helps themselves. Amen. Say, the Lord provides!"

Annie swatted at her and giggled. "Somebody gone hear you."

"The Lord will part the Red Sea of injustice and send down the manna of equal rights."

"Bill Green don't sound like that." Annie folded her arms.

"Since when you call him 'Bill'?"

"Since when I want to."

Mary's round cheeks dimpled and her teeth contrasted with her purplish black face. "Just think how *Bill* Green would like it if we did something."

"How do you know what *Reverend* Green would like?" Annie whispered pointedly.

"I just bet he would."

▼ ▼ ▼

They dressed to kill. They put on Sunday suits, high heels, and pillboxes. Mary wore her good wig. They put on lipstick and rouge and false eyelashes and drove to town in Mary's Fairlane. They had decided to sit in at May's Drugstore. They parked at the far end of the one-stoplight street, deserted in the cool midmorning. People were at work in the factory, or in the fields, or at the schools. The few people they passed stared at them, but no one knew them.

"Don't you just hate it?" Mary said, seeming to bolster her anger as they walked down toward the store. "If you go in there, the minute you step in the door, ole lady May will break her neck running over to you—'Can I he'p you'—you know, in that syrupy sweet way. She won't let you look around for a second."

" 'Fraid you gone steal something." Annie looked straight ahead down the street of wooden and brick shops. The perspective was broken by the courthouse square and the little brick jailhouse beside it. Annie forced herself to match Mary's determined stride lest her legs tremble so badly she fell.

"Or just *touch* something. And a white person—they can put their hands on anything they want. Pick up stuff and put it back. Like they own everything."

"Lord, you know we better not touch nothing unless we ready to pay for it. Better have the money in your hand." Annie's voice trailed and stopped abruptly when she caught a glimpse of the sheriff's car parked behind the courthouse. What would Bill Green think if she got arrested? she wondered. She thought about the stories she had heard from her uncles, her mother's younger brothers, about spending time in the jailhouse for speeding or drinking. They told about the sheetless cots, the stench of the pee pot, but said that the sheriff's wife's biscuits were good. Annie did not want to try the sheriff's wife's biscuits. She did not want to be dragged out of May's by the sheriff, to be touched by his big hands with the hairy knuckles she had once seen up close when he had come to give a talk at her high school. The thought of being close to him, his chewed cigar and the big leather lump of holster and gun sent shivers through her. But Bill Green had said they should stand up. Bill Green had said that God would send the manna of justice if they would only stand up.

Mary grimaced and balled up her fists as if to force her anger to a boiling point. "White people make me sick. Every last one of them. Sick.

What I'd really like to do is to take ole lady May by her scrawny little neck and choke her."

Annie tried to laugh, but her voice was too jittery. "We're suppose to be *peace* demonstrators."

"I'd like to kick a piece of her butt."

"I don't like her either," Annie said, thinking what Reverend Green might say, "but let's do this the right way. Let's just go in and ask to be served and..." Annie stopped under May's green awning.

"And when she don't?" Mary whispered. "What then?"

Except for the awning, May's was a flat-faced, white clapboard building with a flat roof and a stepped crest. Only one of its double doors opened to admit customers. A bell jingled when they entered. Annie stood with Mary by the door, her eyes adjusting to the dimness, and breathed in a mixture of smells dominated by dust and wood polish. To her right was the cashier's stand with a display of pocket combs, and crowded on long narrow shelves in the middle of the store were goods: bolts of cloth, children's dolls, sewing kits, toiletries, firecrackers, shotgun shells, fashion magazines, and among everything, *The Central*, the town's weekly newspaper. In the back, the RX sign hung from the ceiling above the druggist's counter, hidden behind the clutter of inventory. Along the left wall was a linoleum-topped lunch counter with five backless stools anchored in front of it. It was junked with jars of pickles, loaves of sandwich bread, buns and cake plates bearing doughnuts and pies. The spigots of a broken soda fountain were partially hidden in the clutter. Behind the counter was a grand mirror with ornate framing. It was placarded with menus and handwritten signs announcing "specials." The mirror was grease-spattered on one side from a small electric grill that sat on a shelf. On the other side, two huge coolers stood bubbling lemonade and orangeade. A broken neon sign above the mirror announced, "FOOD THAT PLEASES, FOOD TO TAKE HOME." High above were shelves on which rested plastic wreaths of cemetery flowers.

"She must be in the back," Mary whispered, "else she would've said something by now." Mary stepped quietly to the lunch counter and shot Annie an impatient frown. The scents of bath soaps and powders had attracted Annie as she passed the display, but she dared not touch them. "Maybe we should just buy something."

"What for? You scared?"

Annie straightened. "Do I look scared?"

"Like you gone pass a watermelon. Just do like I do. She gone be scareder than us."

The storage room door behind the lunch counter was open. A low voice came from the room, and suddenly they heard a long moan, as if someone, or some animal, were grieving.

"Jesus," whispered Annie. She pulled on Mary's elbow.

Mary pushed closer to the counter, took a deep breath, and pulled herself up onto the first stool. She sat for a moment, her eyes as excited as a child's on a fairground ride. "You ever sit on one of these?" She caught herself for being too loud. She put on a serious face, her lips folded under so as not to look too big, placed her feet on the shiny circular footrest, and adjusted her skirt.

Annie looked over her shoulder, expecting to see Mrs. May's stick-like figure marching hurriedly toward them, but all was still except for the putt-putting of the ceiling fans.

Mary beckoned to Annie to sit on the stool beside her, and gingerly as a child testing hot bathwater, Annie sat. She pulled herself up on the stool, forgetting to smooth her skirt as Mary had done. She sat ready to jump down at any moment; when the moan came again, she jumped.

"Be there in a minute," drawled a woman from the storage room. It was not Mrs. May's voice, which was thin and whiny. A heavy woman, dressed in a blue calico shift with a lace collar safety-pinned at the neck, stepped from the storage room. Her gray curls were pulled back. Her face looked soft, and her eyes were large and round. When she saw the girls, the woman looked confused for a moment, then she looked frightened and wrung her hands. "May I help ya?" she asked.

Annie looked at Mary, and Mary at Annie. They had never seen this woman before. After a moment, Mary drew a breath and said, "We would like to order." The woman pointed to the menu and stood back as if ready to retreat into the storage room. The moan came again from the room.

"We don't want no takeout," Mary said, growing bolder. "We want to eat at the counter like white folks. We want you to write it down on your little pad and bring us silverware wrapped in a napkin."

"But..." the woman said, and then she blanched. "But..."

The moan came again, loudly. She returned to the storage room.

When the woman came back she was shaking. "I...I can't serve colored."

"Why can't choo?" Mary said. She tried to sound sophisticated. "You have the food. You have the stove. All we want is a hamburger and some fries." She pointed to the orangeade. "And some of that orange drink."

The woman came slowly to Annie. Nervously, she put her hand out to the edge of the counter like she wanted to touch Annie. "I don't want trouble, miss," she said. "I'm just helping out my sister-in-law, Ella May. She's very sick, you know. She's got a gall bladder. I'm not even from here. I'm from West Virginia. I don't want any trouble."

"Yes, ma'am," Annie said, then cleared her throat, took a deep breath, and fought to control her jittery voice. "We just want our rights."

"Listen," the woman said, "I will give you some food if you'll just take it on home." Then she added in a whisper, "Mr. May will be back from the hospital soon and...please..."

"No," Mary said firmly, crisping her endings the way their English teacher Miss Bullock had told them was proper. "We done come all the way from Washington, D.C. We are part of President Johnson's civil rights committee. And we gone report you to the Doctor Martin Luther King."

The woman stepped back from the counter. She bumped against the ice cream box. She seemed not to believe Mary but was too afraid to say otherwise. "Mr. May will return soon," she said, too uncertain to be threatening. She strained to see out the front door. Annie knew she was looking to see if somebody white was out there, and spun in a sudden fright. Two black boys were brushing hayseed from their hair in front of the window.

"If it were up to me..." the woman said. "If it were up to me, I would be glad to serve you. I don't mind colored. Honest. I'm from West Virginia."

"It *is* up to you," Mary said, a crooked, dimpled smile on her face. "Who else is here? How come you don't want us Negroes to have our rights?"

"Please," the woman said, clasping her hands together, "I don't want to have to call the police. Don't make me call nobody." She strained again to see the street.

The moan came again. No one moved. They let the moan and the putt-putt of the fans bathe them. Annie felt the moan in the pit of her stomach. She held onto the seat of the stool. Maybe Mrs. May was dead, she thought, and someone was crying. They shouldn't be causing this trouble if Mrs. May was dead. "Well, maybe we should come back when Mrs. May is here," Annie said vacantly, all the time moving a little ways down the counter, focused on the crack in the doorway to the storage room. She could only see a bare lightbulb and switch cord and cans on the shelves.

"I'm not taking a step until I get served," Mary said. "I don't care if Miss May—if the owner—ain't here. You in charge and I want my rights."

The woman put her hand out to Annie. "What if I made you a nice sandwich and you can take it with you? I'll let you have it free of charge."

"Ain't that some mess?" Mary said, putting her hands on her hips. "You even *give* us food, but you don't want us to sit and eat it like people. You rather see us go out back and eat it like a dog. I know how you white people is. I done seen it. You have your damn dog eat at the table with you, but you won't let a colored person. Do I look like a dog to you?"

"I don't own a dog," the woman said. She no longer wrung her hands but gripped one inside the other. "I don't own this place. I'm just helping my sister-in-law like I told you. And besides, it is the law. Like I told you, I got nothing against you. Not in the least. But what would Mrs. May or Mr. May say if they walked in here and I was letting you eat? They wouldn't like it."

"I don't care what they like. The customer is always right."

The moan came again, this time discernible as a word: "Maaahhma."

"What's that?" Mary asked, her eyes wide.

"It's nothing to you," the woman said.

Annie saw a movement, a shadow, behind the door. It was a slow, awkward swaying. The door squeaked and moved slightly. Annie looked first at Mary and then at the woman.

"I'll tell you what *is* my business," Mary said. "This here piece of pie is. And I got a good mind to help myself to it right now." She reached out for the lid of the pie plate.

"Don't let me have to call somebody."

"Call who you like. I ain't scared. I'll go to jail if I have to."

"Don't be ugly," the woman said and waved her hand. She might have been snatching a fly out of orbit. "Just take it and go."

The moan came again, deep and pathetic. It reminded Annie of the mourning doves that she could hear from her bedroom window just after sunrise, only it was not so melodic as doves.

"Go!" the woman shouted. "You're upsetting him."

The shadow swayed again, and the door, squeaking, was pulled open farther. Annie moved closer to the door, directly in front of it, separated from it only by the counter gate. She knew there was someone there, some "him" the woman had said, but something monstrously sorrowful and she couldn't imagine what it was.

Mary hopped down from the stool. "I told you I wanted it here." She jabbed her finger on the countertop. "Why don't you admit it? You just like every white person I ever seen. Just as prejudice' as the day is long."

"I'm not!" the woman said. "You don't understand the position I'm in…"

"Maaaaahhhmmaaa."

"I'm coming." The woman made a step toward the door, then she turned back to Mary. "I'm not prejudice'." Her face was contorted. The moan came again, with a resonating bass. "Baby," the woman said to the figure behind the door, and then to Mary, "eat here, then. Eat all you want. I don't care."

Mary stood stiffly, smiled. There was a small silence. "Serve me," she demanded.

"Serve your goddamn self," the older woman said, her voice rising to a screech.

Annie heard the argument, and glanced now and again at Mary and the woman, but now the door was slowly swinging open, and she could see the thick fingers of a man holding onto the edge of it. He was a big man. Big and fat like the sheriff. Annie looked at the woman. She felt her lips part. The moan, almost a groan, vibrated in her chest. The man was like an animal, a hurt animal, calling for his mother, Annie thought. Now she was afraid in a different way. She remembered what her father had told her about hurt animals, how they turned on people who tried to help them, how their mothers attacked ferociously to save them.

"Serve yourself." The woman had turned toward Mary. Her entire body trembled, her hands, now unclasped, fanned the air. She pushed a loaf of sandwich bread across the counter toward Mary. She slapped a package of hamburger buns, causing it to sail and hit Mary on the shoulder. She threw Dixie cups, plastic forks and paper napkins. Mary ducked below the countertop. "Serve yourself," the woman screamed. "Eat all the goddamn food you want."

"Maaahhma."

Stepping cautiously as if walking up to a lame wild dog, Annie slipped through the counter gate. The door pulled all the way open and the man stood there. Annie's heart skipped a beat; she reached back for the counter so she wouldn't fall. First she saw his barrel chest, bulging out in odd places under a pinned-together plaid flannel shirt; then his thick neck, stiffly twisted so that one ear nearly lay against his hulking shoulder. His lips were thick and flat. One side of his face was higher than the other, like a clay face misshapen by a child's hand. His eyebrows were thick ridges that ran together at the top of his wide flat nose.

"Maaaaahhmmaaa."

"He's just a baby," the woman came to the door and took the man's hand. She pulled him into the open, behind the counter, and rubbed the back of his hand furiously. His presence seemed to calm her. She glanced toward Mary and then to Annie. "It's the new place." She smiled as if inviting a stranger to look at an infant, then shot a look at Mary. "He's not used to being over here." She patted the hand and the big man smiled deep dimples. She pinched his cheeks. "Just a baby."

"What's wrong with him?" Annie asked, recovering from the sight of him.

The mother sighed. "Just born thatta way, child. Just born like that." She looked back at Mary who was straightening her clothes and wig. "Maybe we'll all sit and have a piece of pie."

The man smiled at Annie, and Annie managed to smile back. She reached behind her for the counter gate.

"Don't worry," the woman said. "He is as gentle as a fly. He likes to be around people." She changed to baby talk. "Don't you, Willie?" Then she held out the man's hand to Annie. "Here. Pat the back of his hand. That's what he likes."

Annie looked at his face, drool in the corners of his mouth. He had gray eyes that swam lazily in their sockets. Now she looked at the offered hand. It was the whitest hand she had ever seen, with thick, hairy knuckles and nubbed nails.

"Go on and pat him," the woman said."He's just a boy—your age. Go on, he likes it."

She had never touched a white boy. She reached out for the hand hesitantly. The woman encouraged. Annie wanted to look at Mary, to see what she thought, but she could not break her focus on the man's hand. She saw her hand, so obviously brown, move into her focus, and then move closer and closer to the pale hand until her fingertips touched it.

"Go ahead and give him a pat."

The man's hand was soft and damp, unlike any hand Annie had ever touched. She lifted her hand and patted the big hand twice, and then twice again. The man moaned, not any word but like a dog enjoying a bellyrub.

"See," the woman said. She looked at Mary. "See. We are just people like you are. We don't want to hurt nobody. Not a soul." She took back the man's hand and smiled at Annie. "Tell you what. I'll cut us all a piece of pie."

"Can we have it at the counter?" Mary glared at the woman, her lips poked out.

The woman sighed loudly. "Won't you understand?"

"Then eat it by yo'self."

The woman turned to Annie and touched her hand, "Won't *you* understand?"

Annie hesitated. The doorbell jingled and Mr. May came in. He was wiping under his straw fedora with a handkerchief. "I'll be glad if that old witch did die," he was saying as he made his way to the back.

Mary spun around and pretended to be interested in the bath soaps. "You being he'ped?" he asked gruffly as he approached her.

"Yes, suh," Mary said.

The woman was trying to push the man back into the storage room. Mr. May stopped and put his hands on his hips. "Damn, Sally, what is he doing out in the store? He's liable to scare somebody to death…and what!…in the hell is that gal doing *behind* the counter?"

"It's all right." The woman turned and waved Annie through the counter gate. "She was just helping me with him."

"Look at this place? What the hell happened here? Goddamnit, can't you control that freak?"

"It's all right," the woman said from inside the room where she was pushing the man. "Y'all run along now."

▼ ▼ ▼

"That wasn't fair," Mary said as they walked back to the Fairlane. "How come that stupid gorilla had to be there? How come *she* had to be there in the first place? Ole lady May the one I wanted to be there. I could have said something if it hada been her." Annie said nothing.

They passed the monument to the Confederate dead, standing in the courthouse yard.

"I don't know," Annie said. She was beginning to tremble on the inside. The world seemed complex and uncertain. She remembered touching the man, her brown hand against his white one. He was like a baby, soft and damp, and yet something about him, not just his size and his twisted face, frightened her. But she had been charmed by him for a moment, charmed by his softness and his dimples. She remembered the look on the woman's face when she had patted the man's hand. She thought the woman had loved her for a moment.

"We never gone get our rights." Mary clenched her teeth. "Especially with you around pattin' that goddamn monster on the hand."

"What was wrong with that?" Annie said. She knew there was nothing wrong with it. He couldn't help the way he was born.

"If you don't know...!" Mary reached out quickly and pinched Annie on the arm just above the elbow. She squeezed her nails into the pinch and twisted it before she let go. "Some civil rights marcher you is. Bill Green will be 'shame' to know you."

Annie whimpered and put her hand over the pinched spot. "No!" she blurted, "I *want* my rights."

"Shit." Mary took Annie by the elbow and led her to the car. "I know you was tryin'...I know...it's just that we won't ever get nothing, nothing—unless we, we...uggghhh!"—she grimaced—"*kill* them, or something."

They reached the car and got in, then Annie began to cry. Mary touched her hand to comfort her, but Annie pushed her away. Mary sped the car out of town on a road that cut through fields turning brown in the hot autumn sun. Annie put her head on the dash. Things were very complicated, far more complicated than she had ever thought.

# How I Got My Personal Politics

I wouldn't say that Izella was that bad-looking. True, she wasn't no knockout, even though sometimes she pretended she was a movie star or something. She was always complaining about her hair because it was short and brittle. She tried everything to get it to grow and ain't nothing worked. Like one time when we were sitting in the lunchroom at the factory where we did piecework, I told her, "Izella, if you'd just leave it alone—grease it up good and twist some paper rollers into it, and put on a scarf for a couple of years"—I didn't mean to say years. It just slipped.

She rolled her eyeballs at me and kept on eating some Sugar Babies—with that comb hanging out the one side of her head, the other side snaked with stubby plaits.

"Izella," I told her, "go ahead and get yourself a 'fro. Stop ruining your hair—the little bit you got left—with the hot iron, and just make yourself a 'fro."

She rolled them eyes. "Naw, I don't like no Afro. Colored people got they heads nappy enough as it is. They don't have to make no style out of it. Besides, it ain't gone do nothing in here but catch lint like a sieve."

"And pressed hair don't catch lint? Girl, you be looking good with a 'fro. Looka that girl, Cicely Tyson. She got herself a good style."

"Humph, all that nappy stuff waving all over her head. She probably got roaches living in it. Besides, I hate it when they get 'em flat on the back or on the sides from sleeping on 'em, and they stick all up like a anthill or something. Girl, I want to look good. I don't want no mess on my head a comb couldn't get through. I want some nice locks like Ann-Margret or Diana Ross. Did you see her hair on that album cover? She got good hair—be hanging right down her back. She can swish it out of her face and make a ponytail with it. Or anything."

Lunch bags rustled as everybody packed up their Tupperware and their folded waxed paper. "That's *her* hair. You got to work with what you got."

Izella's eyes watered. "Ain't it a damn shame," she whispered. "God gave white folks everything. Money, houses, cars, good hair. Ain't gave poor black folks a damn thing."

"Diana Ross ain't white." I didn't care who heard me. "Neither is none of the Supremes."

"I can see," Izella snapped at me. "But I bet Mary Wilson wear a wig. That's what I believe and that other girl do too, 'cause every time you see a picture of 'em, they got a different length of hair. But Diana must have some white blood in her somewhere."

"Shiiiit."

"It's the truth. 'Cause ain't no colored person got hair like that by hisself!" She was leaning across the table when the buzzer rang.

"That may be so, but it don't matter. Even them with good hair still black. Some of them think they ain't, but they is."

She looked at me kind of funny—I reckoned because I got pretty good hair. Then she rubbed her fingers across her own frizzy hair. "I need myself a perm." She sighed like a movie star and fluffed at her hair. "A real good perm so I can get some curls in this mess. I'm tired of the straightening comb 'cause it just leave your hair limp and greasy. I want a light feeling. I want it to bounce and fall around on my neck. You know, like Elizabeth Taylor or somebody."

"You mean you want to be white." I said it for a joke.

"I ain't said that. You didn't hear me say that."

Mr. Levine came strolling by the lunchroom door. That was his way of rushing us. "That's what it sounds like you're saying," I whispered as we hurried back to our machines.

"I did not say the word 'white.' I'm just as proud of being colored as you is. And I'll come up side your head if you say different. All I said was that I wanted good hair. Wanting good hair ain't wanting to be white. It's just wanting to be...to be pretty. That's all."

"I'm sorry," I said. I started my machine. The machines all around us began to hum. Up and down the lines, the cone-shaped spools of thread began to vibrate and the different colors of thread fed jerkily into the machines. Fine sprays of oil and lint dust began to fog the air so that the far side of the plant got right hazy.

"Girl," Izella called to me above the noise of her machine, "I've got to do something with this head. I've got to get me a perm. Even if I could just get half-good hair like yours." She stopped her machine and stared straight ahead like she was looking at something on the other side of the plant that she couldn't see. "If it kills me, Ruth," she turned to me, her face contorted, "I am going to get a head of good hair."

▼ ▼ ▼

Patricia Jackson, a girl who works on line C, said her sister Beatrice fixed hair in Richmond and could do perms, and we could go down sometime and get our hair done for half-price. Just say Patricia sent us. When we went, we got lost and ended up getting there after the shop was closed. I said maybe we could get something to eat and come back next month.

"Uh-uh," Izella said, her voice shaking with hurt. She jumped out of the car even before I turned off the motor and ran up to the door and knocked anyway. She knocked three times and turned to look at me with a look so hopeless it scared me. Then I saw a dim light come on in the back and a shadow move behind the window, which read "Bea's Unlimited Beauty Supply and Salon." Handwritten signs advertising "Press and Curl" and "Perms" were taped on the inside. I pointed to the window and told Izella to knock again. She rapped on the window and a girl who worked there opened the door for us. We told her who we were. Her name was Peggy and she seemed real nice.

"It's a shame y'all drove way down here and can't get no perm," she leaned against the doorjamb, smoking a cigarette while she talked. "But Beatrice done gone home and I think she is going out to the Eastern Stars tonight, so she won't even be at home."

"Well, at least I enjoyed the ride," I told her. The sun was setting. Cars were putting on their headlights. Their tires made a sticky sound as they moved through the damp streets. Men were going in and out of a bar across the street. Heavy R & B thumped when they opened the door. A group of boys was coming home from a baseball game. The smell of frying meat was coming from somewhere. Izella started to cry. "Just seems that everything goes against me. This was my one big chance to get my hair done up nice and now I can't even do it 'cause somebody so countrified she can't even drive in the city."

"I can drive all right," I said, "when I got the right directions."

"You woulda had the right directions if you hada took 'em down right."

"I did take them down right." We fussed about the directions for a few minutes, Izella getting real shiny and snotty.

Then Peggy moved aside from the door, letting us in. "I ain't suppose to—cause I ain't got my license, but I can give you a perm. It's real easy."

Izella's face lit up. "You know how to do it?"

"Yeah, just follow the directions on the back of the tub. My boyfriend is coming in a little bit, but it don't take long."

"You done it before?" I asked.

"I done seen it done. But Bea don't let me do nothing much. Sometimes she let me wash somebody and sometimes she let me roll somebody, but mostly she just make me sweep the floor."

Inside were two rooms, smelling sweet like Dixie Peach. In the front room were two chairs, one with a dryer behind it, the other next to the sink. Hair magazines were stacked on a coffee table. On the walls were pictures of women, some of them white, modeling hairstyles.

Peggy set up for the relaxer, pulling a big jar with an eaten-away label from a bottom cabinet and placing towels around the sink. Then she sat Izella down in front of the sink, put tape on the back of Izella's neck, and taped a plastic sheet over Izella's forehead and face. Izella undid her hair, which stood up over her head like the rough insides of a horsehair mattress.

"My hair ain't too bad," Izella whined, hoping we would agree. Peggy just grunted, but I said, "I done seen worse."

Peggy, wearing rubber gloves and a mask, scooped whitish goo out of the jar and rubbed it into Izella's hair. The smell of it burned our noses and made our eyes run.

"Whee-ew." Peggy turned up her nose. "Is it burning you?"

"That's all right," Izella said. She sounded happy.

"You tell me if it's burning you. This stuff will burn if you ain't careful. It ain't suppose to stay in but a minute. I think it's made of some kind of chemical like lye."

"That's OK as long as it gives me that silky look."

"Oh, it will do that!" Peggy, popping her gum, was slicking the white paste over Izella's hair, which was plastered against her head. "It's working already."

"Oh, let me see!" Izella jerked her head, and Peggy told her to lie still lest she get the relaxer in her face. I got the hand mirror and held it for her, but she couldn't see for the plastic over her eyes. Izella squirmed with joy. "I can wait. And I don't care much if it does burn me. I want to have good straight hair, and if I got to burn a little to get it then I'll just burn."

Peggy agreed. She said that a little burning meant that it was working. "But don't let it get too hot. I'll leave it in ten minutes, but if it gets too hot, then I'll have to wash it out."

"You can leave it in for a whole hour if it gone make my hair good. Child, I can't tell you how long I been wantin' to get good hair."

Peggy sealed Izella's hair in a plastic cap. The goo seeped out around the edges.

"You just wipe any of it off with the towel and I'll come back in a minute to put in the neutralizer and wash it out." Peggy started toward the other room, the office, and then she turned to me. "You want me to give you one too?"

"That's all right," I said.

"Lawd, thank you Jesus!" Izella said, her eyes hidden by the plastic and her mouth just one big grin. "This is just a miracle after all." She touched the plastic cap like she was afraid it would burn her. "Is it getting straight yet?" She squirmed.

"I can't see it for the cap," I said.

"It feels like it's getting straight. Lawd, lawd." The big grin was on her face again, then she started putting on airs. "I just don't know how I'm going to fix my hair this evening, darling. Shall I wear it with a little flip to the side, like Petula Clark, that girl that used to sing 'Downtown'? No. I know exactly how I shall have it, darling—like Jackie Kennedy, just straight and stylish, coming down over my ears and flipping in toward my mouth on both sides. Then I can flip it to this side"—she moved her head slowly so not to throw off the cap—"or flip it to that side. And if a strand of it falls down in my eyes I can just blow"—she pursed up her lips and blew—"and it would just fly up and fall back into place. Or maybe I would just leave a big ole curly lock hanging over one eye like Ann-Margret—that would be so sexy. But then I'd have to color my hair. I should dye my hair while I'm here. I'll make it red—no, blonde. Gentlemen prefer blondes. And then I can pile it up on my head like Debbie Reynolds. You see the way she puts her hair up? I wonder who does her hair, anyway? It always look so clean and shiny—like she has nothing to do all day but to comb her beautiful hair and tie it up in silk ribbons and drink champagne and eat caviar."

"It's supposed to," I said. "She's a movie star. You reckon it's been ten minutes yet?"

"It ain't been five minutes yet."

I went to the office to find Peggy. She was on the telephone, talking real soft, and gave me a look like she didn't want to be disturbed. I went back out into the parlor. Izella was scratching a little at the cap.

"Is it burning?" I asked.

"It's getting good and hot." She was smiling. "But that's all right. It's just doing what it's supposed to do."

She talked a few minutes longer about hairstyles and fashions and what kind of makeup and jewelry would go with her hairstyle. I was paging through a book on hairstyles that had a lot of women in there with hairstyles called "The Beehive," "The Cleopatra" and "The Goddess."

"It's getting kinda hot now," Izella announced. She had a painful grimace on her face and she was wringing her hands.

Peggy gave me a mean look when I came in. When I didn't leave, she put her hand over the mouthpiece of the phone and said sharply, "I am on the phone to my boyfriend."

"I'm sorry," I said. "But I think it's time for that stuff to come out."

"Is it hot yet?"

"Yes."

"I'll be there in a minute."

I went back and told Izella, who was beginning to fret. She was fanning her head with her hands.

"Let me take it out," I said.

"You don't know what you're doing."

"I know you' burning up."

"I can stand it a minute longer." Sweat was rolling down her cheeks.

I went back to get Peggy. She had lit a cigarette and was blowing out a cloud when I opened the door. She looked at me like she was going to kill me. "She's burning up," I said.

Peggy said something nasty into the telephone, and then she said to me, "Just wash it out then," like she could care less what happened to poor Izella. I didn't leave. I put my hands on my hips to show her I meant business, but she turned her back on me and mumbled angrily into the phone. Then she turned back to me and flicked her old, dirty cigarette. "I'll be there in a second."

"She'll be *dead* in a second," I said, turning away. When I went back Izella was crying.

"Shiiiiit," I said. I ripped the cap off her head and stuck her head under the running water. She screamed, and her hands came up to fight me.

"You don't know what you're doing," she cried, trying to hold onto my wrists so I couldn't keep her head under the stream of water. The water began to wash the gunk out. It ran down the drain in a white swirl. But as it washed out, big clumps of Izella's hair washed out, too. The sink became black with strands of her hair and the drain began to clog.

Izella stopped fighting me. "Is it straight?" Her voice was half-crying. "Is it straight? Is it straight?"

She lifted her head and saw herself in the mirror. The stuff had burned her hair right down to the root. In places there was nothing but bald scalp. She opened her mouth to scream, but she didn't say anything. She didn't even cry. She kept rubbing her fingers across her bald head, like she was trying to run them through long hair, and every time she made a pass, more of her hair came out.

Then Peggy came into the parlor. She was saying something about men. She stopped when she saw Izella. "Good Lord!" She turned to me. "You done ruined that girl's hair."

▼ ▼ ▼

Izella didn't kill Peggy, but she tried. At first I felt like holding Peggy so that Izella could beat on her, but I broke them up instead. I greased Izella's head with Vaseline and loosely tied a scarf around it. I told Peggy that I would make sure that Beatrice heard about it and that Peggy would be lucky if she ever got another job in the beauty parlor business. Then she got uppity and kicked us out of the shop, saying she was just trying to help us and this was what she got.

I had to lead Izella to the car the way you lead a blind person. She was so ashamed she couldn't hold up her head. When she sat in the car, she put her head down in her lap, and if she lifted it up, she would duck if she thought somebody was looking at her. When we got to the corner of Boulevard and Broad, which are two main streets in Richmond, she looked up and saw a shoe store and a wig store all in one.

"Oh," Izella screamed, scaring me, "that's what I need. I need to get a wig." Her nose was stuffy from crying. "I can't go around with no scarf on my head." We didn't have money for any wig, but we got out and looked in the store window anyway. The store was called "Artistic Wig and Shoe." It had wigs of all colors, with long or short hair. We thought that one of the shorthaired wigs would be less expensive, but when we got inside we found out that the cheapest one was a long, curly blonde one.

A long-nosed white man came over to sell it to us. He had been sitting behind a counter, smoking a cigarette. I had smelled the cigarette, but I hadn't seen him for all the wigs and heads and shoes stacked on the counter. It was one of those old stores with squeaky wood floors, a long middle aisle, and boxes and boxes everywhere stacked up to the ceiling.

"Can I help you girls tonight?"

"How much for that wig?" Izella pointed to the wig, even though she knew what the price was.

"The price is on the ticket."

"I ain't got that much," Izella said to me, but loud enough for the man to hear.

I looked in my purse. I had ten dollars and I gave it to her to add to her twelve. Still we were three dollars short.

"This is all we got," Izella pleaded.

"But this is the price." The man pointed to the ticket. "I can't make any money if I sell below what it costs."

"Oh, please," said Izella, "I had an accident with my hair." She indicated the scarf.

The man rubbed his palm together. "Ummm," he said, "what kind of accident? Let me see."

"Let's get out of here." I tugged on Izella's arm.

Izella started to leave. Then she pulled away from me and said, "What do you want to see for?"

"See if you really had an accident," the man said. "I can't believe everybody that comes in here claiming they had an accident so they can get a free wig." He was leaning on a stack of boxes, half smiling.

"Let's go." I gave Izella a hard tug on her arm. But she was untying the scarf and jerked her arm back. She was breathing hard, and just before she took off the scarf, she hesitated.

"Come on, Izella. We can find another wig."

She snatched the scarf off her half-bald head. "See!" she declared to the man. "See what happened!"

The man let out a soft whistle. A smile cracked around his lips. He slapped his belly but he did not laugh out loud. "Well, well, well. How did you do that? Did you do that trying to control your hair?" I could tell he was choking down laughter. He shook his head, the smile still trembling around his mouth. Then he took the wig off the dummy's head and handed it to Izella and took our money.

Izella put on the wig the moment we got back in the car. She adjusted it and put the curls all around her shoulders. "Who do I look like? Do I look like anybody?" She was looking at herself in the rear view mirror.

I couldn't say anything. I tried, but I couldn't think of anything to say. All I could see was this shiny mess of curls reflecting the traffic lights.

"I look like Marilyn Monroe?"

Then I said, "I can't tell. It's too dark." That was all I said. I didn't even look at her when I said it.

Izella got quiet and looked out the window. She stared out at the passing lights until we were way out in the country, halfway home. She put her face in her lap. "Stop. I'm going to kill myself. Stop the car." I pulled off to the side of the road, scooted over to her and took her in my arms. We both cried.

# The Lighthouse

## 1. The Lighthouse of Deliverance

The church is humming. In the choir stand Sadie Bales is going crazy on her tambourine. Richard Bales is banging on the piano. He is just making it up, but the church is loud enough to half drown him out. Reverend Peach is prancing across the altar. He is mopping his brow with a white handkerchief. I can see his initials in the handkerchief: little t, big fancy P, little c.

His voice is hoarse. He says, "God is calling his children home. God is calling! God is saying to his children this morning that he loves you and that he wants to hold your precious souls in his hands." He cups his hands, the handkerchief inside like a little cottony soul. "He wants to cradle your soul." He slurs when he says "soul." "God is calling!"

Now he is hunching his shoulders. His face turns sour. "But God is like any good father—he calls you, but he disciplines you, too." He slurs again. "Brothers and sisters, if you don't know him on earth, He will not know you in heaven." His body is shivering from the quaking spirits. His hands fly up, the handkerchief is waving like a white flag. "Hallelujah!" he says. Then he is jumping, his knees together. He comes down off the altar and is walking among the congregation, not saying anything but quaking and looking like he is about to weep.

Ruth Hankins shoots up from her seat. She is shaking every ounce, her big underarms beating the air as her hands make a frenzy of praise.

"The spirit is here! God is right here!" Reverend Peach is shouting. He is stomping out a circular dance. Richard Bales is picking up the rhythm on the piano. Sadie Bales is getting happy.

Sadie's head is jerking so much that her hair ball flies loose. Mildred Johnson grabs her by one arm so that she won't fall. Sadie knocks over a choir chair. Sister Bishop grabs her by the other arm, but the spirit is catching. It runs from Sadie right into Sister Bishop and Mildred finds herself holding onto two happy women.

Sister Bishop's daughter, Ilene, takes Sister Bishop by the shoulder and sits her down. Sadie knocks over two more chairs before she is finished. Nobody cares. They say let the spirit have His way.

It is quiet. Everybody is catching a breath. Sadie is sitting, her arms folded, her eyes closed. She is rocking, saying, "Thank you Jesus thank you Jesus thank you Jesus thank you Jesus thank you Jesus..."

Reverend Peach is a handsome man and he knows it. He is not built like other preachers. He is big, but he does not have a fried-chicken gut; he's got muscles like a muscle man. He wears a white tie and white shoes. Holiness people don't believe in preachers wearing robes. But he says it is all right for women to wear lipstick as long as they don't make themselves look like Jezebels.

He is calling up Reecy Perkins. He says, "The Lord is calling, calling, calling out to his people. The Lord is saying to old Satan, 'Let my people go.'" Reecy is switching up to the altar. She looks like she is embarrassed at being called. She is a Jezebel, and everybody knows it.

Reverend Peach is laying on hands and shouting at the devil in her. She is switching in a different way now. She is feeling the power of the Lord. Reverend Peach is speaking in tongues. He is shaking like a man in the electric chair. Sweat is pouring out of his head. When he jolts the sweat showers off him.

Reecy is crying. Sadie is happy again; now she is speaking in tongues, shouting one word over and over. Everybody is standing, shouting praises and dancing except for my nephew, Junebug. He is walking out the back door. Something is going to happen to him. I'm scared for him. I can feel the power of God. It is stiffening my hair and brushing against my skin.

Now Reverend Peach is walking to me. He is holding up his hand for the church to quiet down. Bales stops playing the piano and says, "Take your seats, if you can. Please, take your seats, if you can. Reverend Peach has the word of God."

Everyone settles except Sadie. Mildred is nudging her to shut up.

"Speak. Let us hear the word," Papa is saying. It is the first time Papa has said anything except "Hallelujah" since we came in. Junebug is like Papa, quiet. When I get a furlough from the hospital, the others act like they are happy to see me. Junebug acts like he is 'shamed of me. He really thinks I'm crazy. He is scared that we may have something in common.

Reverend Peach's big handsome hand is reaching out to me. I know what the Lord is saying is about me.

"Brother Otie," Peach is saying, "do you love the Lord?"

"I reckon so," I say. "He has been good to me."

"Thank you, Jesus!" I hear my sister Phillipia say, half singing. She closes her eyes, but she does not look like she is praying, more like she is hoping.

"The Lord has a blessing for you. The Lord told me to reach out to you and offer you His blessing. His is the blessing of eternal life. His is the blessing of salvation. Do you believe the Lord can deliver you, Brother Otie?"

"I *know* the Lord can deliver me. I have been praying that the Lord would see a way to deliver me," I am saying. "For truly, I have sinned and transgressed in His sight. I know the Lord is a merciful God, and that is why I know that he can—no! That he *will* truly deliver me from my sins and transgressions which are many. For lo, I have walked in the valley of the shadow of death. Lo, I have walked side by side with evil, and I know if it hadn't been for the Lord Jesus Christ that I would be dead and gone and buried in hell."

A murmur is rising. Ruth is waving her arms in a frenzy. I am feeling a charge coming up from behind me. I pop to my feet. I am feeling the Lord working on me. I want to talk. I want to tell all my sins. I am saying whatever is coming into my head. I am saying that I am a bad sinner. I say you don't know what manner of evil the devil has laid upon my heart to do. The devil has asked me to take all kinds of drugs and even to kill. The devil has told me to kill myself, and if it wasn't for the goodness of the Lord, I would be dead and burning in hell right this minute.

"Mercy, mercy, mercy," I hear Phillipia saying like she is ashamed. Now I am feeling cold and silly so I stop. The church is moaning. They are on the verge of exploding. All they need is one sign from Reverend Peach and they will rock the aisles as they have never been rocked. Reverend Peach's face is contorted like a baby getting ready to cry. He doesn't believe me.

"The devil told me to kill a man," I am saying. "He showed me how to do it and put it in my heart to do it. When I was in Petersburg, he told me. He told me just how to put a pillow over a man's face and to lean against it. Then the man would grab your wrists and try to wrestle, but you just lean and he can never get up."

"Mercy, Otie," Phillipia is saying. I turn to look at her, and I see Junebug standing in the back, beside the door. He is shaking his head. Reverend Peach is shaking his head. Papa is looking down at the dust on his shoes. Phillipia is looking up, eyes closed, hands clasped together under her chin. Silently she mouths the name of Jesus.

"Humph, humph, humph," Ruth Hankins is grunting.

"What a pity, what pity, what a pity," Sadie Bales is saying.

I start to sit down, but Reverend Peach is growling, "Stand up!" His face is twisted and hot. His lips are spread open on just one side of his mouth so that a gold tooth with a star in it shows. His eyebrows are buried down in his scowl. He is grabbing me by the shoulders and he begins to pray in tongues. He lets go of my shoulders and then he does his little spinning dance like he is a spring winding up. When he is tight, he pauses and taps me on the forehead with his sweaty palm. It is a light tap, but I fall out. Nobody can catch me; I can't stop myself. I hit the bench and roll out onto the floor, but I don't feel hurt. I can smell the dust from the floorboards. I can see Reverend Peach's sky-blue knees. I can see right up his crotch and beyond to his hot face which seems swollen like it might be filling the ceiling. The lightbulb is crowning him from behind so that he looks like he is wearing a halo of fire.

I feel the floorboards bounce up and down. Dust is rising around my head. It seems that everyone is dancing, except Reverend Peach.

"In the name of Jesus," he is saying, "I cast out demons." He is reaching into my shirt pocket and taking out my cigarettes. Cigarettes fall about my head. "I cast out Demon Alcohol. I cast out Demon Thief." He is stamping his big shoes right beside my head. I feel like if he would hit me, it wouldn't hurt. "I cast out Demon Liar." He goes on casting out my demons, and the church dances and dances harder each time one is cast out. I am lying where I fell. I cannot move. It feels good. I feel the demons leave me one by one, hissing out of my ears, tickling them like tongues, prickling my lips like little kisses. When Reverend Peach says, "Liar!" a big one leaves.

▼ ▼ ▼

I have five dollars and a quarter the church collected for me—and not a single cigarette. Papa and Phillipia are getting ready to take me back to the institution. I can hear Phillipia inside the house hollering at one of her cats. I stand on the porch and look at Junebug strolling slowly by the flower patch. He looks like he is walking through a world of thick air. He is good-looking, but he doesn't believe it. He has no meat on his bones. He is a college boy, Phillipia's pride.

"Junebug!" I call, stretching out the "June" part. "Run me up to the store. Junebug!"

He looks up like I scared him, and says nothing for a minute but keeps staring. His shoulders draw back like he wants to fight. "For what? Cigarettes?" He looks like he is sucking lemons. I don't have a chance to say anything and he gives me the fuck finger. If it had been a shotgun, it would have killed me. Then he walks off and won't look back.

I look at him walk away and suddenly I want to kill him. I see the ax standing straight up out of the chopping block. I see myself running through the flowers, swinging the ax over my head, swinging it at Junebug. I am swinging for the back of his heart, right between the shoulder blades. I hear it smack him. I see the blood.

Then Phillipia comes out of the house and puts her hand on my shoulder. "You ready?"

I stiffen. I try my best not to move.

## 2. Deliverance from the Lighthouse

Peach hates me. He hates college boys. He knows I've found him out. All I know is booklearning, he'd say. What he knows is divinely inspired. If he takes one good look at himself, he'd see that his prance, his blue suit and white shoes, and his embroidered hankie do not make him look smart. Next, he'll say that divine inspiration led him to his divine bad taste.

Nonetheless, he is handsome and he knows it, and this congregation, full of overweight old women, is swooning over him. My mother is among them.

They say they are full of "the spirit"—as if there could only be one. They say they are the chosen few, they are the God-awful saved ones, but I have seen them in anthropology films. They are the same as fire-eaters, hot-coal walkers, and tree divers. Just as primitive, just as backward, and just as self-important. These Negroes are much nearer the tribe than they ever dreamed. Maybe there is nothing wrong about it. A lot of stuffed shirts could do with a little wallowing. Myself? I just wish they weren't so damned self-righteous. Their motto is "I've got my Jesus, now you get yours." I'll tell you what my Jesus is, Sir Reverend High Chieftain Peach: dope, booze, and sex from anything that will lie down.

My mother, Phillipia, breaks my heart. She is an attractive, chestnut-colored woman, well kept for thirty-eight. Thus far, she has fought off the pounds that swell country women, rounding them softly then broadening their hips until they can barely sit two to a pew. Ruth Hankins, I predict, will be dead in a year. They'll say heart trouble killed her—or high blood pressure—the common excuses. But it will have been ignorance. Ignorance of diet. Ignorance in faith.

Now Peach reads my face. He says that book knowledge will not bring you to faith. Faith is taking God at his word. Faith is leaping blind, as Abraham took his only son Isaac to the altar, blind of God's plan. Book knowledge corrupts. (He overlooks the logical fallacy that the Bible is a book.) It is a tool of Satan. Don't get me wrong, he says. He looks at me. Does he want an "Amen" from me? He says book knowledge will harden the heart and make a man too proud to know God. A man must know God as a little child. Now he stomps the altar with his big white-shod feet. He shakes his hands like a haywire maniac. Quaking spirits.

He has charisma. I'll give him that. He has got rhythm. He is infectious, if you don't listen to what he says. He is convincing, if you don't look for his witch doctory. Even Phillipia is under his spell. She is doing a graceful little hop, like a robin. Her hat falls off. If I do testify, if I would dare, I would say that every handsome man—including Christ—is not your savior.

I count fourteen women, some of them teenage girls; five men: my grandfather, a middle-aged man, assistant to the almighty Peach; two teenage boys, assistants in training; a crazy man, my Uncle Otie; and me. We are Negroes with a little "n". "Negroes" said with a smirk by certain of the better bred, high-toned. We are scrub people, ill bred, poorly educated, and graceless. Yet there is salvation, for I am not as graceless as the rest of them.

Peach is uttering his trash, building toward the show stopper. It is high theater, tragi-farce. He is making his metaphysical connection, building tension for shenanigans. My marrow aches; I believe he will choose me. I stand and make my way out the back, and as I reach the door, the tension eases a little. The sacrificial lamb is chosen; it is poor Otie who will be going up for his ninety-ninth healing.

I peep through the crack of the door. Peach sees me. He will confront me later.

Otie is standing and facing Peach. Otie is as big as Peach, but he is soft. He is graying badly. Next year we will say he is old. Today we only say he looks old. He is clever though. He answers Peach word for word.

"Do you love the Lord?" Peach asks.

"I reckon I do," Otie answers. He has the simple logic that only a crazy man could have. He is as calm as a pond, yet something boils beneath the surface, something fierce and perhaps dangerous. The question is, can he play Peach as Peach intends to play him?

The congregation is on edge. Everybody is murmuring. A few are getting ecstatic. The woman in the choir pews, the pianist's wife, is going through her routine. She is a melodramatist, all performance and no substance. The others lean forward, and the garish colors of their polyesters swim in the frenzy of their swaying. A fuzziness blurs them, the way the horizon is blurred and yellowed before the rain breaks in an electrical storm.

Peach is too quiet. He is standing like a judge. The church itself will swell and its whitewashed blocks will explode, its creaky wooden floor will splinter, will warp, will whirl from under us if he does not move. Soon he must condemn the devils or lose his audience.

Otie confesses to innumerable crimes. He is getting older by the second. He is losing his touch. He probably believes himself now. He confesses to theft, to lies, to murder. It is time for him to shut up, and mercifully he does.

Now it is Peach's turn. He catches my eye. He is saying, "This one's for you, you little mouse. This will be you when I get ahold of you." He winds up like a cartoon character and socks Otie with the power of God. Hold out, Otie. Sock him right back. Tell him to wave his magic wand somewhere else. Otie falls like he is made of cardboard. Peach looks at me again. He could be smiling. "See? This is real. This is the real power of what I can do, you worm." He winds up again. "I've got one for you, too." I turn away. I want a cigarette. Old Otie is a buffoon. He has been crazy for twenty years.

Perhaps I, too, would have fallen like a feather, would have surrendered to the power of that man, would have groveled for salvation. Many times I have gone up to that very altar, Phillipia and Hankins behind me like sisters of mercy, while Peach pumped the power of God into me. I remember I was fifteen and more afraid than anything. Have you ever come face to face with God? But in those days the power of Christ was exciting to me. It promised to make the unseen visible. It was the energy of light, the glistening God of action, the handsome living entity of God. No bloody-handed effigy; this God was purity and power in action. He was the dashing crusader, God the swashbuckler. All I had to do, they said, was to believe—but how can anyone simply believe?

I see Otie, the crazy man, the most sensible of us all, swept from his feet like a ball of lint. He lies as if taken into another world while the witch doctor rebukes his demons.

In weeks to come, they will tell it like this: Peach threw out Otie's demons. Demons rose out of him one by one. They will say: the room got ice cold. Hair stood up on heads as Peach cast out the devils. Horns rose out of Brother Otie's head, and Reverend Peach touched him and lightning struck the devil down. Saying it, I suppose, is half of believing that good triumphs over evil.

When Otie is up again, when the commotion quiets down, the Holy Rollers get down to the real business of religion——collecting money. They take up a special basket for Otie, who is newly washed by the spirit but must return, nonetheless, to the funny farm. The choir renders a selection—or rends it. The poor and the hopeful drag themselves up to cast their last pennies for God. Even the choir members hobble down from their perches, still squawking, and place money in the wicker baskets. Peach sits like a pharaoh, his eyes alight as if he were breathing oxygen from another world, and fans himself with a portrait of Martin Luther King. He is watching me. "I've got your number. One day, brother worm. One day, bow down."

Even I do not dare begrudge Peach his dollar. At worst, he's been a dollar's worth of entertainment. But I will not put a cent in Otie's basket.

▼ ▼ ▼

We are back home and I have escaped the inquisition. Peach had his fan club to contend with, and Phillipia rushed us back so that she and Grandpa could return Otie to his rightful keepers, the state. That is the greatest blessing this family has ever had. I am walking among Phillipia's giant zinnias, appropriately called "Old Maids." Otie is on the porch, doubtless itching to spend his fortune.

"Junebug," he calls to me. Junebug is no longer a name I'll answer to. It is the worst misappellation for Junior I have ever heard. "James to you," I mumble.

"Juuuuune buuuug," he calls again. He wants me to take him to buy liquor or cigarettes. He was saved for all of thirty minutes, delivered from his sin by the Lord incarnate Peach at the Lighthouse of Deliverance Soul-Saving Mission.

Suddenly I am ready to fight. For a heartbeat, I could kill Otie. I turn away and walk straight through the zinnia bed, breaking the stalks and stirring the bees. He calls again. I look behind me. I see him on the porch, a shrinking man. I see the house, a white box, a mimosa in the yard. The sky behind the house is pure and blue. A perfectly white cumulus cloud throws its shadow on the house. All above is perfect; all below…

I realize that there is no one to kill.

# Sweet Milton

Milton is my new friend now. He has beautiful feet. I say to him, "Milton, you got some pretty toes. They so clean after you get done with your shower. You put some baby powder on them and they smell like roses. And they ain't hairy toes like I seen on them white boys. You keep your nails trimmed neater than anybody else here, and you ain't got no awful big feet like mine. You ain't got no crooked baby toes like mine."

He says, "Get out of here, boy. Don't be bothering me about my feet. If you want somebody's feet, there're plenty that will give it to you. You see Lillie?" He leans back in the upper bunk so I can't see him. "Lillie's got plenty of toes to show you."

Milton has good hair. He keeps it parted and slicked to one side. He trims his mustache down to a pencil line and lets it ride the crest of his lips. His lips always look wet and soft. Sometimes he will put on a little lipstick so his lips will look red and pretty. Lillie will give him lipstick almost anytime he asks for it. She says her husband gives it to her and it's the only thing he ever gave her that she wanted.

She gives the lipstick to Milton in craft therapy. She is painting a paint-by-number of Jesus knocking at Martha's door. She uses yellow where it says to use blue. Miss Grafton does not like it. She says she will tell Haggerty. Lillie does not answer. When Grafton goes away, Lillie tells me that Jesus' robe can be any color it wants to be. She says Grafton is a long-nosed bitch that ain't never been to church, much less seen the color of Jesus' robe. She says she is going to ask Sister Jacks what color Jesus' robe is. Sister Jacks looks into the wall. She starts to hum. She is looking at Jesus. She says that his robes are yellow as sunshine.

Milton asks if it's before or after the Ascension, and Sister Jacks does not answer. Then she says, "Yella, yella. Gold like de street of Jay-ru-say-lum. Hi-lay-loo-ya!" She claps her hands. It is powerful clapping.

"Quiet, now!" says old Grafton. "Quiet or you'll have to go back."

"Yea, do I walk in de vale of death, thy evil touches me not. For righteousness does faller me all my good an' earthly days." Sister Jacks points to Milton, "Git hence me devul. Hence me, now."

She is humming now and gluing a shell on her candy jar. She glues one shell every day. She may finish the jar this year.

Lillie is painting Jesus' hair green. I tell her she is not staying inside the lines. She says she is giving him a new hairstyle. Lillie kicks off her slippers and I say, "You have beautiful feet. I never saw such beautiful feet before."

"I have heard that lie before, Mr. McPhee. All men do is lie to ladies. You know they are ugly feet."

Grafton tells me to get to my project. My project is an ashtray. It is the twelfth ashtray I have made this month. Milton says one day I will get it right.

▼ ▼ ▼

We are in the ward, singing. Milton is singing the blues. He is singing, *Git up, Momma. Git up off yo' big fat rusty-dusty. Oo-oh, git up, sweet Momma. Git up and be good 'n' trusty.*

I am singing the gospel. I am singing "Love Rescued Me." Milton joins the chorus after awhile. He says I have a way with the gospel. Then he whispers to me to look at Bernard beat off.

"Pull on it," he says to Bernard.

"Go 'head 'n' pull it hard," I laugh.

Bernard turns over so we can't see him anymore, but he won't stop pulling. Fred Hanks says Bernard is heading straight to hell.

"Where do you think you are?" asks Milton.

"I ain't in hell," says Fred.

"You look like you are in hell."

"You don't even know what hell is." Fred stands up. "You don't know nothing about the Bible. You are a sinner and the Lord will visit his wrath upon you."

"You in hell, boy. Hell. You in hell. You in hell. Hell. Hell. Hell."

"Then who the devil is?" asks Fred. "Tell me who the devil is?"

Milton leans back in his bunk, which is up and across from Fred's. "You want to know? You really want to know?"

Fred is dancing up and down in the space between the bunks. He pokes his tongue out at Milton. "Mr. Smarty, who the devil is?"

Milton asks me for a Camel and we both smoke. Bernard gasps and starts all over again. Fred settles down but keeps laughing, "Who the devil is?"

Just when I am losing faith in Milton, he says, "You want to know who the devil is?"

"Yes, Mr. Smarty. Who the devil is?"

"You don't want to know," Milton laughs. "Otie, does he want to know?"

"I don't think so," I say from down below. "I sure as hell don't want to know." And I really don't.

"Neither does Freddie, baby. Do you, Fred? No, no, no, you don't."

"Yes, I do," says Fred. He pulls his blanket around him.

"No, no, no," Milton says.

I hear Milton stand up in his bunk. I hear him unzip his pants. Then I see a stream of yellow shoot down onto Fred and splash on his bunk and into the space between the bunks.

I get up to look. A Camel is dangling from Milton's painted lips. It's fuming up into his eyes. "I am," he says to Fred. "That's who. I am."

▼ ▼ ▼

C.C. is a big man. He wears a black scarf around his conk. "I'm gone tell Grafton. I don't care which one of y'all done it. Grown man pissin' on de bed."

"He said he was the devil!" Fred says. "The devil." Fred is light-skinned so his face is good and red. "And then...he..."

Fred cannot say the word "piss." He cannot say many words. He stamps his feet into the pool. "He said...he...oooh, he wet on me!"

"You make dis mess?" C.C. asks Milton.

Milton is smoking a cigarette. He answers slowly as if he is just waking up. "You talking to me? You know better than to ask me such a silly question like that."

"He is...he did...he did." Fred is shaking his head. "He said he was the devil!"

C.C. wallops Fred across the face and tells him to shut up. He says if Fred doesn't shut up he is going to see that Haggerty fries his brain. "I be making sure smoke come outta yo' ears."

Milton and I laugh.

C.C. goes over to Bernard and asks him who did it. Bernard doesn't say anything. "Mr. Burruss, kin you hear me today?" C.C. is talking like Grafton, like a grown-up talking to a boy.

"Yes," says Bernard.

"Did you see who made dis mess?"

"Yes."

Milton sits up in the bunk and glares at Bernard.

"Den tell me who done it?"

"You better tell the truth," Milton says, "or somebody's going to get you. Somebody real big—with horns and a tail."

"Shet up!" says C.C.

"And a pitchfork."

"Who done it?" demands C.C.

"Yes." Bernard shakes his head.

Milton is laughing.

"Who done it, Mr. Burruss?" C.C. is trying to be nice. "Who done it?"

"He did…he did…he did. He said he was the devil and then he did it."

"Shet up," C.C. says to Fred.

"Yes," says Bernard.

"Sheeeet!" says C.C. "You bunch of goddamn nuts."

"Just be a good boy and clean up the mess," Milton says.

"Shet up."

"Don't tell me to shut up." Milton puts his legs over the side of the bunk and cups his thing. "I got something you like."

C.C. don't say anything. Then he kicks Fred's feet which are still in the pool of pee. He sees me in the corner and yells at me. "Git back in yo' bed, you buggy-eyed ass-licker." I start to move. Then he says kindly, gently, "Maybe you seen who done it?"

"Of course I did," I say. "The devil done it."

▼ ▼ ▼

Fred is sleeping from a pill the night nurse gave him. Bernard is snoring. I can smell Milton smoking from his secret cigarettes because C.C. will not let him smoke after lights-out.

"Milton," I say, "are you awake?"

"No, stupid," he says. "Go to sleep and let me think."

I let him think for a minute. "Milton," I say, "I want to ask you something."

He does not answer. Then he says, "What, stupid?"

"Do you really believe that you are the devil?" He looks over the side of the bunk. All I see are his eyes, upside down, and the red butt of the cigarette.

"What do you think?"

"I don't think you are," I say. "But I think you might be possessed by the devil."

"You got it wrong," says Milton and he swings back up. "I am the devil. I am not possessed by the devil. I *am* the devil."

"Then why are you in here?"

"Why do you think?"

"I think you are because you think you are the devil."

"No, no, no," says Milton. "I know what I am. I know what you are, too. And Fred, and Bernard, and C.C. I know all about all y'all. I know what y'all done and how y'all going to pay for it. You know you got to pay—and Grafton, and Lillie, and old Jacks, and Haggerty, too." He let the hand with the cigarette fall over the edge of the bunk. "Stick with me and you won't pay too bad. Don't stick with me and it will be pure hell."

"It is not hell," I say. "It is a good place. A place to get myself well."

He gets out of the bed and puts his pretty foot on my chest. I can't see the foot but I can feel the straight toes digging into my chest. I touch the foot and I feel the smooth skin and the ridges where the skin runs over veins and bones. I try to bend up and kiss it, but my lips won't reach. Then Milton chuckles. "It's as close to hell as you will ever get."

▼ ▼ ▼

"The moon is pretty tonight," I say to Lillie. She backs up against the fence.

"When did Milton say he was gonna come?"

"He says not to wait for him. He says that he is everywhere like a spirit. He says he is in the grass like a snake. He says he is in the corners of the roof like a wasp nest. He says he is really the devil."

"Shhhaaah!" Lillie says. "I know what he says. I know what he wants you to do." She folds her arms and looks at the moon. "He says it is my punishment for being mean to my husbin." She begins to cry. I touch her shoulder. Now she is sniffling and she wipes her wet face against my hand.

"I wanted *him* to punish me."

I take my hand away and look through the wire fence at the town lights below us. I can almost see the outlines of the roofs in the moonlight. "This certainly is a high place to be hell."

"This ain't hell," she says. "It's just a nut farm on a mountain."

She pulls down her panties and lies in the grass. "C'mon, let's git it done; it's cold out here."

I don't even unbutton my pants but just put my thing out through the zipper. I have to pull it to make it hard and then Lillie and I do it. She gets carried away after awhile and rolls over on top of me. I am looking at the moon and then I am satisfied.

Lillie is crying again. She hasn't bothered to put her panties back on. I want to go again if she will do the work. She says she has been punished enough. She keeps crying.

I ask if this is the way she was mean to her husband.

"Yes," she said. "I did it with everybody except him. But he was...," she sobs, "so ugly to me."

I told her what I had done. I had loved a boy and deserted him when he got hurt and couldn't love me back. "You should never desert someone who loves you," I say, "no matter what. That's what God wants us to do."

She is sobbing harder. "I don't believe in love," she says. Then she pushes me to the ground and starts humping on top of me even though I am flabby. I can't tell if she is laughing or crying.

Then I hear C.C. coming along the fence. He sees us and clangs his billy club into the fence.

"What de shit, Otie?" he says to me. "What de shit is dis?"

I am trying to get up. He pushes me down with his foot. Lillie rolls off of me and he pushes her down to the ground by putting his foot on her head.

"Dammit," I say and try to get up again. He cracks me beside the head with the stick and I see stars. Now I am facedown and trying to get up and he cracks me across the shoulders with the stick.

"What de shit is dis?" he says. "Run away? Rape? Lawdy, lawd, boy. They gone fry yo' brain."

"Don't...fry my brain," I say.

He pushes me with his foot. Lillie gets up and jumps on him from behind. He screams. She is biting his neck. He smashes her in the chest with his elbow and she falls on the ground beside me.

He swings the club back like he is going to wallop us both. Then I see Milton standing behind him. Milton lets out a stream of smoke so long that he must have been sucking it up from hell.

"C.C., ease up," says Milton. "Ease up."

"I knew *you* had ta be 'hind dis," says C.C.

"Let 'em go."

"Sheet!"

"Let 'em go, C.C., and we can talk some business."

C.C. hesitates.

Milton lets his pants fall down to his ankles, and leans against the fence. "Y'all go on back," he says to Lillie and me. "Y'all been punished good enough for tonight."

# The Bottoms

Parthenia Mills had made a reputation for herself in the Bottoms as hardworking by day and fun-loving by night. The churchgoers tolerated her. They spoke politely when they saw her, but behind her back they shook their heads in wonderment as they gossiped about how much she drank or which men she entertained. The partygoers did not like her. They found her sometimey: sometimes she wanted to party with them, and sometimes she didn't. Many a man, in the late night, sweaty from dancing and warm with liquor and marijuana, had wobbled up the dark stairs to her small apartment, only to find himself being pushed down the stairs in the morning and told in a short, cutting voice, "Nigger, don't ever show yo' black ass 'round here no more."

As she often did on Saturday evenings, Parthenia stood on her narrow balcony and looked out over the square tarred roofs of the Bottoms. In the streets the young men were gathering. They stood about in groups of two or three. They laughed and slapped hands together and saluted passersby with the power fist. A sultry Motown song spilled from a tattered Buick as it crept along the narrow street. A teenage girl, too hip-heavy for the short skirt she wore, made excited gestures toward the Buick's driver. The driver wore a scarf around his conk. He seemed oblivious to the girl. His cigarette smoke curled lazily out of the window as the car passed slowly by. Parthenia knew the man had noticed the girl. She knew that he didn't take his one red eye off her. She knew how it felt to be under the gaze of that eye. She tightened her grip on the balcony railing. Two years earlier, the driver, called Redeye, had killed her lover.

She retrieved her dress from where it aired. No breeze stirred outside, but the evening was dry and comfortable. She made a bath in the sink, pressed the edges of her hair with a hot comb, and slipped into the dress. It was not a fashionable dress; she did not like them so short as all that. But it was a dress that accented every curve of what it covered. The material was sheer and cool. The pattern was a pink floral, and the dress was cut low along the shoulders and breasts. It buttoned up the front, and Parthenia left the top button open.

She went to the mirror and dabbed rouge on her cheeks and smeared on lipstick. She did not rub the makeup into her skin but let it lie on her round face like a veneer. Noticing a stray hair in the thin line of her eyebrow, she took up a straight razor and scratched it out. The razor felt cold in her palm, and she held it a moment longer than she needed to. It had belonged to Harold, her lover. "Never you mind," Harold would tell her often, "one day we gonna move out of the Bottoms. We'll move to the top."

"Just like in the movies?" she asked coyly. She wanted to believe him but worried that he was too big of a dreamer. Before they moved to the Bottoms, they had lived in another project, and another before that.

"Just like in the movies," Harold replied.

She walked back onto the balcony. In the dusk, the dinginess of the Bottoms seemed disguised; the squareness of the buildings was softened. On the ridges surrounding the Bottoms, the lights from the downtown skyscrapers glimmered. She closed her eyes and imagined what wonderful things occurred downtown where gentlemen escorted ladies to the theater or to expensive restaurants. She wished. When she opened her eyes, it seemed that the Bottoms had been transformed. It was no longer the Bottoms but an enchanted place.

At Dick Spooner's, a juke joint, Parthenia bought herself a half-pint of High Ten and a beer chaser. She found a good table in the corner and poured the whiskey into the paper cup and drank. By the time the square room had become crowded and smoky, she was drunk and happy. She spoke loudly to two women whom she knew by sight but whose names she never remembered.

"What y'all up to?"

"Look who talkin'," one of the women answered. She wore a blonde wig.

"You gone speak tonight, ain't cha?" the second woman said, smoke fuming out of her mouth.

Parthenia swung one shoulder in a way that let the criticism roll off. "Don't I always speak? I thought I did. If I don't, y'all, it's just 'cause my mind is busy with some shit. My mind is always busy."

"Her mind be sloppy," the second woman remarked to the first. "Her mind be—look a here, I say, her mind be so sloppy her momma be mopping it up with a rag."

The women laughed loudly, and Parthenia laughed with them.

"That's a good one!" Parthenia cried out. "But at least the people be diggin' my groove. They be saying, 'She a right-on chick.' They don't be turning up their noses because somebody's momma ain't taught her how to wash under her arms."

"Who you talkin' 'bout?" the blonde asked defensively.

"Don't the shoe fit?"

Before the woman could answer, the music struck a deep blues chord and Parthenia danced into the center of the room. Her dance was slow and sinuous. She churned from side to side, rolling her head and running the fingers of one hand over her hips. Her eyes were closed and the tip of her tongue showed through the crack in her lips. Before she had finished her dance, she felt someone standing beside her. Opening her eyes, she found a young man whose light skin seemed to change colors under the blinking party lights. He smiled at her. It was a gentlemanly smile, something she hadn't seen since Harold died.

"You're a truly groovy dancer," he said. Then for a moment he looked unsure of himself. He pushed his wire-rimmed glasses back up on his nose. He wore his hair in the new Afro style, and he wore a dashiki instead of a shirt.

"You're a college boy!" Parthenia blurted.

"I'm a college man."

Parthenia put her cup to her cleavage. "Sure 'nough? I be diggin' myself some college man."

He and Parthenia sat at her table in the corner. He had a pint of Southern Comfort that he had sneaked in. He offered some to her.

She accepted the liquor before she realized what it was. "Where did you get that? You ain't supposed to bring your own in here. You supposed to buy it from Spooner."

"Spooner won't mind," the boy said with bravado, but slipped the bottle into his waistband under the loose dashiki.

Parthenia swirled the liquor with her finger and licked it. "You're cute. What did you say yo' name was?" The boy's name was Lincoln Williamson. He was a Morehouse man. He had finished one year and had stayed on for summer school.

"Call me Linc."

"That's a funny name."

"It's for Lincoln."

"Like Abra Ham Lincoln."

"Right on, sister."

"He freed the slaves." She sipped the drink and gave the boy a coquettish smile. "You gonna free me?"

Linc leaned on his elbows and studied her face. It was a little too round and sad but beautiful despite the ravages of the drink. "Parthenia." He looked about cautiously. The barroom was noisy, bustling with figures shifting and dodging through the blinking party lights. "Are you cool?"

She straightened herself and pushed her chest out. "Of course I'm *cute,* fool. What do you think?"

"No. *No.*"

"What the shit do you mean 'no'?" She started to stand, but he caught her hand and held her.

"No. I know you are *cute.* You are very attractive. You are the most attractive young woman in this place. In fact, I have never seen a woman as good-looking as you anywhere. That's why I came over here." The flattery stayed her. "What I was saying is, 'are you *cool?*' Do you smoke pot?"

She did not answer. He was not sure she had heard him.

"Pot. You know, marijuana. Grass."

"Oh," she said. "Herb. Yeah, I smoke herb. If it's good shit and don't give me no headache."

"It's good."

She stared blankly for a moment. She could hear her heart thumping in her ears. She realized he still had his hand on hers. It was a lean yellow hand with a ring on the little finger. Harold had worn rings, one on each hand. He had had long fingers like the boy's, only he had been much darker. She took her hand away and coyly put it to her mouth. "We could go up to my luxurious apartment," she said slowly, "and we could smoke." He grinned.

She pulled him through the crowd toward the door, making certain that they passed before the table of the women to whom she had spoken earlier. She lingered before the table, making sure that the women took notice of her and the boy.

"Looka there," the woman with the cigarette said. "Don't take her long to get her a piece."

"I don't reckon so, if you go down every time de wind blow. Be going down in de middle of the street like some ole bitch dog in heat," the blonde said.

The other woman rolled her eyes at Parthenia. "She be doing like a dog, bent over and humping in de bushes, in de street, in de alley, anywhere. She don't care."

Linc blushed. He realized the conversation was about Parthenia and, by association, himself. "Young ladies," he said, as if to scold them, "don't belittle your sister. We are all the same people."

"Who the hell is this college nigger?" asked the blonde.

The other woman mocked him. "We are the same—listen to what I say—the *same* peoples. You don't look like Martin Luther King to me."

"Lawd, girl, maybe he think he a preacher or something. Maybe he one of them talented ten. Maybe he number nine."

"Nah, girl, he just one them stuck-up college niggers think he Jesus Christ."

The blonde put her hand to her mouth and mugged a shocked expression. "You done used the Lawd's name in vain." Barely hiding behind her mock seriousness, she studied Linc and turned back to her friend. "He don't look like Jesus Christ, either. Jesus Christ be white."

Parthenia put her hands on her hips and slunk between the boy and the table. "Don't pay no attention to them. They're just jealous. Just as jealous as little mouses that ain't got no cheese."

The blonde threw back her shoulders. "Honey, I done had me a college boy, and they ain't that good."

"I reckon so," Parthenia said coolly. "One whiff of you would kill anybody." In one motion she snatched the blonde's wig and sent it scooting onto the dance floor to be trampled. The woman put both hands to her natural hair, brittle naps rolled in brown paper. Her mouth made an "O", but no sound came out. As quickly as that, Parthenia pulled Linc out of the door.

▼ ▼ ▼

A sliver of yellow moon hung above the rooftops, and the streets were lit only by the scarce light from windows. The boy stumbled as Parthenia dragged him along the broken sidewalk.

"You ain' drunk, are you?" Parthenia asked. There was a slight cutting edge to her tone. "I don't like my men drunk. Can't do nothin'."

Linc pulled back for a moment. He wanted to go with her; he found her provocative, yet he did not want to be dragged along the streets by her. "Who says I'm your man? Suppose you're my woman?"

Parthenia leaned against the stucco wall of a storefront. Music from Dick Spooner's came around the corner. "Uh-uh, sugar. I ain' nobody's woman no more. You hear me? And if you don't like it, you can turn your yellow butt around and go on back up the hill where you belong."

"Now, Parthenia," Lincoln sighed, "what kind of way is that for a sister to talk to a brother? Ain't you hip to the revolution? No matter what color we are—yellow, brown or black—we're all African people."

"I ain't no African." Parthenia had heard that kind of talk before, mostly from the college students she encountered in her job as a maid at a motel. The students talked about brotherhood and sisterhood and about how all black people should unite. It was easy to talk revolution when you were on your way to college. Linc was the first one of them she had ever seen in the Bottoms.

She leaned into him and rested her head on his shoulder. She felt one of his hands on her waist and the other one slip across her ribs and stop under her breast. Her pulse quickened. She held her breath. These hands reminded her of Harold's, and she wanted to dream that they were. "Just like in the movies?" she thought. "Just like in the movies." Suddenly she pushed away from the boy and looked him in the eyes. "Listen, you are just my overnight man. You hear? This thing is just for a night." He smiled at her. The sight of his white, even teeth made her shiver. She wanted him to sweep her off her feet and take her away. "Maybe it ain't a good idea." She found it hard to breathe. He looked so much like her lover. "Maybe you ought to go away while you can."

"Now why would you say a thing like that?" Linc put his hand on her breast. "We could be so beautiful together."

She laughed quietly. "Don't fool yourself. You don't know where you are."

"Does it matter?" He put his mouth next to hers.

The liquor on his breath still smelled sweet. His soft cheeks brushed against hers. She felt as though her body might become liquid.

"God, girl, you turn me on. You're so goddamn sexy."

"That's right—as long as it's just sex, it's all right." Again she leaned into him and allowed him to put his arms around her and they kissed. Her tongue tasted the inside of his mouth. It was the first time she had kissed a college boy, and she allowed herself to dream. Suppose it were more than a one-night affair. Suppose he fell in love with her, respected her, and took her out of the Bottoms. She couldn't hold the dream in mind for longer than a moment.

Harold had spent three months at trade school and was on his way to becoming a certified electrician. She remembered how he had changed toward her. He still talked about leaving the Bottoms, but now he criticized the way she dressed, the way she walked, her drinking. He corrected her grammar. He didn't want her to talk to certain people and thought she should associate with certain others. The closer he came to climbing out of the Bottoms, the more she felt he was leaving her behind, and the more she had resented him. Then he made his fatal mistake. He forgot he was still in the Bottoms when he crossed Redeye.

The car did not surprise Parthenia. She had heard it purring as it crept down the street, and when it was close she loosened her embrace on Linc and led him along the sidewalk. It was Redeye's Buick. It slowed as it approached.

"Just keep on walking and pay him no mind," Parthenia whispered to Linc whom she had felt tighten at the approach of the car. Redeye peered out the window. He was a very black man whose left eye had been damaged in a fight. He had taken off his scarf and his hair lay hard and close to his skull. The gruffness of his bass voice startled Parthenia. He called, "College boy."

"Don't pay him no 'tention."

"College boy," Redeye called flatly and beckoned.

A cold spot came into the pit of Parthenia's stomach, though she knew she had no reason to be afraid.

"I'm talkin' to *you*, college boy," Redeye growled.

"What you want?" Parthenia snapped.

"College boy." The engine stopped and Redeye stepped out of the car.

"What's happening, brother?" Linc extended a hand. Redeye pushed the hand aside. He was wiry and shorter than Linc, but he carried himself like a big man.

"You go back up the hill where you belongs and don't come here no more. I catch you at Spooner's messing with our girls, I'll hurt you."

"Hey, brother, we are all the same people."

"Where is it?" Redeye demanded suddenly.

Linc stuttered for a moment. "Where's what?"

"I ain't a fool, boy. Spooner said you snuck in liquor. Give me the bottle." Redeye put a finger in Lincoln's chest and Lincoln pulled the half-empty bottle from his waistband.

Redeye chuckled. "What is this shit?"

"It's groovy stuff, man."

"Groovy stuff?" Redeye repeated. He looked at Parthenia. "What is 'groovy stuff'?"

"He's just a boy. Leave him alone," Parthenia said, almost in a whisper.

Redeye held the bottle above his head and in a quick, smooth motion threw it to the concrete. Linc's face flushed. His jaw ticked. Redeye saw the anger and stepped back. Broadening his shoulders, he let his hands swing loosely at his hips.

"Leave him be, Redeye," Parthenia said. She gave Linc a gentle nudge toward the ridge. "You better go on."

"No," the boy said. "I'm not a scaredy-cat if that's what you think. I belong here just as much as you do. You don't own the street. I got a right to be here."

Redeye stood still, intently watching the boy's every move.

"Go on, goddamnit," Parthenia urged. "Go on before something happens."

"Nothing's going to happen," Linc said.

"I don't care then." Parthenia shook her head. "It's you now. I told you to go and now, it's you."

"You heard the lady," Redeye said.

Linc glared at Parthenia. "What do you mean, it's me? I thought we were in this together."

"No, lover." Parthenia shook her head. "I'm alone." She started away, wobbling a little on her high heels. "Thanks for the tricks!"

Linc lunged at her, caught her by the arm and spun her around. "You can't just walk off. What do you think I am? I may not be from down here, but I'm somebody too."

"You may be somebody somewhere, but you ain' nobody here," Parthenia said and jerked away. He caught her by both arms and shook her. "Listen, sister, don't leave me like this. I'm...I'm a *brother.*"

Redeye stood behind him and gently, as if nudging him with a finger, put a six-shooter to the back of his neck.

"Bro-tha," he mocked, "let's see what you got." Then he told Parthenia to take Linc's wallet and to take out the money. Then she took his watch and the medallion from his neck. Linc breathed hard through his clenched teeth.

"You don't like this?" Redeye said to him. "I ain't want you to like it. You college boys think you own the world. This here is the part you don't own. You dig? You ain't slick enough for the Bottoms. You dig? Answer me."

"Yeah." Linc's glance caught Parthenia's and she could see defiance in his eyes. It frightened her. Suddenly he seemed dangerous to her. She took a step back but could not escape his eyes.

"You caused it," she said to him defensively. "You should of stayed up there. You had no reason coming down here and messin' with us."

Linc cursed her. Redeye pressed the old revolver deeper into the base of his neck, but as he did so, Linc stooped and spun behind him and the two men wrestled. In the brief flurry all Parthenia saw was the flail of arms. When they stood up, Redeye held Linc's head under his arm and held the gun with the other hand to Linc's temple.

"What is it?" Redeye growled between heaves of breath. "What you want me to do? Kill 'im?"

Parthenia stepped back until the wall of the storefront stopped her. "Kill 'im?" Redeye asked her again. Wave after wave of tingles swept up her spine. She wanted to run but could not. She wanted to look away but could not. Once before Redeye had asked her that question. Then he had had a straight razor to Harold's throat. Then her tongue had quivered, and she didn't answer. Now it seemed her breath had completely left her. What was this boy to her, anyway?

"What will it be?" Redeye twisted Linc's head so that Linc faced her.

His pupils were so wide she couldn't tell what color his eyes were. He didn't look human anymore.

"He's just a boy, Redeye. He don't know nothing."

"You want me to let him go? He be coming back around here?"

"He won't be coming back, Redeye. He learn' his lesson."

Redeye considered for a moment. "I don't think so. This punk think my dog ain't got no bite." He twisted the muzzle back and forth against Linc's temple. "But my dog got a bark and my dog got a bite. But my dog ain't never had a bite of college ass." He looked at Parthenia and demanded, "Do you want me to kill him, or do you want him? You can have him for Harold. That's what you been looking for anyway, someone to take Harold's place."

Parthenia's heart fluttered. He could never replace Harold.

"Please, goddamnit," Lincoln said.

Parthenia heard him but did not consider him. She looked up at the scythe of a moon that hung above the flat roofs of the Bottoms. It seemed romantic and dangerous. She felt herself tingling, alive and beautiful.

"Kill 'im?" Redeye's breathless question came again.

Parthenia pushed herself forward a step. She threw the money and jewelry at Redeye's feet. "Kill him," she said. "Kill him, if you want to." She started to walk away. The further away she walked, the more the tingling subsided. She heard the Buick's engine turn over, and relaxed. Then a shot went off and echoed from square wall to square wall throughout the Bottoms. Parthenia froze. Then she took a deep breath of Bottoms air. What was the boy to her? She decided to go home and take a bath. Even if Redeye had killed the boy, what was a college boy to her?

# Flora Devine

During the perilous days of segregation, the Crossed Bars was a rowdy, blue-collar lounge frequented by aging WSB radio stars and Ku Klux Klansmen. The radio stars, people like Fiddlin' Tom Benson and Peewee White, hung around the front of the long bar that ran right down the middle of the large square room. The bar was a rectangle with a narrow island in the middle which held all the liquor and glasses. In the back, away from the windows, the Klansmen met. No one bothered them, unless summoned. In the front were pictures of country-and-western singers, both the local WSB performers and famous ones from around the country. In the back, barely lit, hung a Confederate flag.

But new times had come, and little was left of the Crossed Bars clientele. The only ruckus the old men who now populated the bar caused was an occasional beef over a game score or a pinch to the rear of one of the women. The women knew how to handle rough play. It was the kind of place where a woman did not wear a dress.

Flora Devine wore a dress. Joe, the bartender, looked up when she came in. He did not take his eyes off her for a moment, but not because of her color. Black girls, usually prostitutes, came in all the time and caused no trouble. And not because she was pretty. Though neatly dressed, she was middle-aged, and had a plain, worried face. He stared because she seemed strange to him. Sad. Sad eyes. Sad mouth. A sad stooped, slow walk. Even her hair, held by bobby pins, seemed to lie as if someone shaken by grief had styled it. She made him nervous.

"Can I help you, ma'am?" Joe said. He was in his late twenties, a business college graduate. "Ma'am, can I help you?"

Flora came to the bar, across from Joe, and said nothing. She stared past him into the dimly lit back of the room where the flag hung. She stared so hard that Joe looked over his shoulder to see what she was staring at. He cast a bemused look at Smith, a regular, and turned back to the frail, watery-eyed woman. "What will you have, ma'am?"

"What's this place known for?" Flora asked. She placed her satchel on a barstool and continued to look around. She had been wandering for two days, looking for a fight. Now she knew she was at the right place. It had an old smell to it, something other than the smell of stale beer and burger grease. It was something ghostly and deadly. Something she had run from all her life until now: she smelled death. It smelled like sweat. Like dust. Like old wood. It made her bones ache. It frightened her.

"She's one of them crazies, Joe," Smith said. "You'd just as soon scoot her on out the door before she causes some trouble."

"She's OK," Joe answered, but was still examining Flora. "She looks harmless. She can sit unless she causes trouble."

"Hell, I'd kick 'er, Joe. I wouldn't give her a chance to put a knife in my back. You heard about that loony down on Ponce de Leon last week? Had an attack and stuck a couple of people with a' ice pick. Nearly killed one of 'em."

"She's OK, Smith," Joe said.

Flora blushed when she realized the men were talking about her. She had been studying the Confederate flag which hung so that its crossbars made a vertical X, like a standing man. "The old rascal," she had been thinking. "Old Mr. Man, old Mr. Dixie himself." She had had plenty of trouble over the years, and in some way, Mr. Dixie had always been there.

▼ ▼ ▼

Her earliest memory of the crossed-bar symbol was seeing it flying on a flagpole at the black elementary school. It was in the mid-fifties, and the state had just changed its Bonnie Blue, the colonial flag, to one that incorporated the Confederate symbol. She asked her teacher why the flag had been changed. The teacher crossed her arms and snorted. "It's a reminder so that you will never forget."

"A reminder of what?"

"What you already know, or will learn soon enough." The teacher had walked away, but her words bothered Flora. A few days later she asked again. The teacher laughed and patted her on the head. "Misery. Misery, my sweet child. Nothing but misery." She laughed again, a high, hollow sound. "You'll get used to it."

From that time Flora saw the crossed bars everywhere, not only on flagpoles but in other places, too. It flew on aerials from pickup trucks. It was plastered on billboards. On television men waved it at the cameras. Every time she saw it, she thought about the teacher. "Misery. Nothing but misery." The teacher had been laughing when she had said it, but even in her laughter there had been sadness.

After she finished high school, Flora attended an all-black college. The college, located in a quiet town, was isolated from the civil rights protests in the cities. To Flora, the movement seemed to unfold at a distance, as though it were an event in a foreign country. She learned about Goodman, Schwerner and Chaney from television. She read about Malcolm X in newspapers. When SNCC or SCLC recruiters came to her campus, she listened and agreed with them and sometimes gave money to the cause, but only once was she tempted to commit to activism.

The day of Martin Luther King's funeral, some of the professors organized a march. A group of about fifty planned to march once around the campus and then across the railroad tracks into downtown. They would stop at the courthouse steps and say a prayer for Dr. King. The march around the campus was successful, but when the group reached the campus gates, it was met by the sheriff's deputies who ordered them back to their dormitories. Flora was at the back of the group and couldn't hear the exchange between the march leaders and the deputies. A cry went up from the crowd, and those at the front turned and began to flee. Flora saw one of her professors holding his head and another being helped toward the infirmary. The march was dispersed so suddenly she didn't panic; rather, it seemed to her that she was dreaming. People moved in one direction, then another, like corralled cattle. She caught a glimpse of a flag, whether state or Confederate she couldn't tell, and for the first time she understood what her teacher had meant about misery.

▼ ▼ ▼

Few people were in the barroom: a black man slumped on his stool to Flora's left; a couple sat in a nearby booth; a waitress, smoking and drinking, shuffled between the tables and the back end of the bar. In the corner, against the wall where the flag hung, sat a solitary man. Flora could not see his face. She only saw his cigarette brighten when he inhaled. Country music played on the jukebox.

"I...I'll...have a beer," Flora said to the bartender, who was just turning away.

"Ma'am?"

"A beer, please."

"You know it'll cost you a dollar and a quarter."

Flora stared stonily. She made a show of taking a twenty-dollar bill out of her purse and flattening it on the countertop. "You don't have anything for twenty, do you?"

"No, ma'am," Joe said, "I just thought..."

"You just thought 'cause I'm black..."

"No, ma'am!" Joe held out his hands to her. "I didn't think that at all. Honest."

"Crossed Bars." Flora tossed her head. "Crossed Bars. You think I don't know what that means?"

"Ma'am?"

"Steppin' Fetchit over there may not know." Flora nodded toward the old black man. "But I know."

"Ma'am," Joe said, "we don't allow that kind of talk in here. Tyroll is a valued customer of ours. We don't go for that kind of name-calling in here."

"What do you go for then?"

"Kick 'er, Joe," Smith said.

Joe considered for a moment. "Ma'am. What kind of beer do you want? We got Schlitz and we got Old Milwaukee."

"That figures," Flora said. "And I wanted me a Colt 45."

"You'll have to go somewhere else to get it."

"I'll have a...," Flora paused to exaggerate her indecisiveness, and then ordered. "The Crossed Bars," she said, emphasizing "crossed." "Do you know why it's called the Crossed Bars?"

"If you've got a problem with it, you can go somewhere else."

"I *do* have a problem with it." Flora tasted the beer, just wetting her lips on the foamy head.

Joe went to the other end of the bar and wiped the counter. Smith shook his head and talked to himself. "Was a time you could come in here—go into anyplace up Ponce de Leon—the Blue Light, MacHenry's, Sam and Dick's—anyplace on Ponce, on North, and things were just nice and peaceful. No foolishness whatsoever. The colored, they had their own over on Dekalb and on Hunter. Nobody bothered nobody. We just had it peaceful."

"Cut the baloney," Joe snapped at him. "You know it wasn't so peaceful. Just a bunch of Cabbagetown hillbillies cutting each other up. And the other side wasn't any better. Isn't that right, Tyroll?"

The old man, half asleep, raised his head from his chest. "Uhh?"

"I said…Never mind."

"Tell me something," Flora called to Joe. "If things are so different now, how come you still flying the old stars and bars? How come you still got them pinned up high so everybody can see? And how come you don't change the name of this place?"

Joe came back to confront Flora. "Say what you want. It's not what you think. Look, you're black…"

Flora made a mockery by looking at her hands.

"You know what I mean! You have a heritage. Well, so do I. And that's part of my heritage. Can't I display my own heritage?"

"That's telling her," Smith said.

Flora smiled and sipped her beer. She felt strong and much happier now than when she had come in. "Listen. That old banner you white folks are so proud of…you know what that means to me? While you calling the name of Robert E. Lee and Jeff Davis, I see nothing but slaves. You know that? *It's my damn heritage, too.* That's why I'm going to go up there and tear it down and *stamp* on it."

"I ain't owned a slave in a long time," Smith said to the couple in the booth, but the two paid no attention.

"What is your problem? What do you want? Nobody in here's done a damn thing to you," Joe said to Flora.

"It's what you stand for." She was enjoying the argument. "It's your system—that flag—the Crossed Bars. You haven't changed a bit. Now, the law has made some changes, but it's places like this that's got to change."

The young man laughed. "Come on, ma'am. We aren't prejudice'. Hell, I believe in justice and freedom for all, just like you do."

The solitary man crossed the room and went toward the door. He was lean and young and looked unhappy. As he reached for the door he studied Flora. Flora could feel him looking at her, but she did not look back. She was afraid; he made her bones ache.

"You come back," Joe called to the man.

The man said nothing and pushed through the door.

The waitress came up to the bar. "That jerk didn't leave me a cent."

"Run out and ask him," Joe said.

"The hell if I am," the waitress turned away. "He was a weird one. I tell ya."

"You get *all* types." Smith rolled his eyes at Flora.

"Don't you roll those bug eyes at me. You don't know who I am. You don't remember me, do you?"

"Me?" Smith said.

"Not you." Flora sneered. "You wouldn't." She pointed to Joe. "Aww, but...you're probably too young. You have heard of Rosa Parks?" Tyroll lifted his head and stared at Flora. "What about Martin Luther King?"

"You mean Martin Luther Coon." Smith laughed.

"Shut up, Smith," Joe said. "Martin Luther King was a great American hero."

"Where did you learn that?" Flora tilted her head at Joe.

"At school. Hell, everybody knows that."

"What do you know about Martin Luther King?" Flora shook her head and sipped.

"I know as much as you." Joe threw the dish towel into the sink. "Just because I'm white doesn't mean I can't appreciate what black people have been through. I have black friends, you know."

Flora let her voice sound flat to emphasize her incredulity. "I'm sure you do. Steppin' Fetchit and who else? Young folks like you who haven't lived through anything yet. I lived through it, you see. So when I say Martin was a good man, I know what I'm talking about. I'm not just mouthing something I read."

"Are you trying to tell me you knew Martin Luther King?"

Flora held the glass to her lips and closed her eyes. She was feeling less happy now. Misery was creeping up on her. She was going to lie, and she didn't want to. On the other hand, she couldn't face the truth just then. She put down the glass and faced Joe. "More than just knew him. I used to march all over Georgia, all over the South."

"You knew him? For real? You helped him? What's your name?"

"Flora Devine."

At the end of a long pause Joe let out a guffaw. "No, ma'am. I'm sorry. I never heard of you."

▼ ▼ ▼

Two years after the aborted march, she moved to Atlanta, and for the first and only time she visited the King grave site. That was as close as she ever got to Martin Luther King. Looking at the crypt with its "Free At Last" message, she shivered and drew close to her husband and baby. Her husband put his arm around her to comfort her. "No," she said, "it's not that." Then she knew she would have a hard time explaining. It was not grief she was feeling but a deeper regret. Remorse. "I should have done something for the movement. Joined SNCC, or marched, or something."

Her husband, a man ten years her senior, laughed. "You'll do well enough just to do well. Raise baby Priscilla and keep food on the table." His smile encouraged her. "There's more than one way to help the movement." She took the baby from her husband's arms and hugged her. She would dedicate this child to Martin Luther King. She would do the best she could to realize in her child the dream King spoke about.

For the next ten years, life went as she expected. She was one of the first black teachers to integrate the public schools. The position seemed an honor. She felt she was helping King's dream come true. But in just a few years after integration, all the white students had moved away. Even though her school remained a good school in a good neighborhood, it became as segregated as before the law had changed. Like the schools of her childhood, the crossed bars flew over this school, too.

Her husband, a Meharry-trained dentist, never established a strong practice. He made the mistake of locating his office in the main shopping mall. Since blacks were deserting the old black business districts in droves to shop in the white-owned mall, he thought the mall location would be perfect for attracting both black and white clientele. However, neither blacks nor whites who came to the mall were looking for a black doctor. Flora argued with her husband that he should move his office to a black neighborhood. The issue became a point of pride for Dr. Devine, and he stayed at the mall until the practice went bankrupt. Unfortunately for Flora, her husband associated his business failure with his marriage and left her for a new life in California. The divorce intensified the gnawing guilt she had about having been complacent in an inequitable country, but worse, she felt powerless, too.

▼ ▼ ▼

Smith called to Tyroll, "You ever hear of 'er?"

Tyroll studied her. His yellowed eyes struggled to focus.

"He don't know you from Eve," Smith said.

Flora took a long drink from the beer and waited for the alcohol to make her feel warm. The effect was slow to come, and when it did, it was not warmth but a slow spinning sensation. Her breath became shallow, and she began to examine her chapped hands. They seemed to belong to a stranger. Smith's laughter was a backdrop to the dense confusion of noises in her own head. What was she trying to prove, wandering around the city looking for a Confederate flag to tear down? Why was she drawn to this place when the flags were everywhere? Dixie this and Dixie that. On bumper stickers. In the newspaper. On T-shirts. Everywhere she turned was a reminder. She thought about her daughter.

"Have you ever had a day...," she mumbled.

"Ma'am?" Joe called to her. "Are you all right?"

"Have you ever had a day when it felt like the earth wasn't moving? You wake up, and the sunlight is not streaming through the window; it's just a bright gray light from an overcast sky. You don't hear birds in the trees. No sound. Not even traffic. Outside everything is so still you think everything must be dead. So you just lie. You lie like you're dead. Whether you lie for minutes or for hours, you don't know. The light doesn't change; there is no sound. Things are so quiet, so still, you think that you have to move. You have to make some noise. So you get up and go to the window. You see that the sky is blue, and you think, 'What a fool, I have been lying up in bed all this time on such a blue day.' But the blue is deeper than sky blue. It's even deeper than the blue-black of storm clouds. There are no clouds, just this deep, flat blue. You look higher in the sky, and you see why. It's not the sky you're looking at. It's a giant flag, and the blue background of one bar. Across the sky, like two high rainbows, are a crisscross of stars." Flora's voice trailed off and there was silence for a moment.

"I told you she was a loon," Smith said.

Tyroll asked Joe for another drink, but Joe ignored him. "Ma'am, can I call someone for you? You got family?"

"Family?" Flora's hands trembled as she pressed her hair against her skull and smoothed her clothes. "I had a daughter. Her name was Priscilla. She was fifteen."

"*Was* fifteen? I'm sorry," Joe said. He had learned in these situations not to ask questions but just to let the customers talk. They would tell as much as they wanted to. He waited a moment for Flora to continue, and when she didn't he asked, "What happened to Priscilla?"

Flora looked directly at Joe. She smiled. Her voice was soft and musical. "She was killed."

Joe leaned toward her. Now she seemed so fragile to him, not at all the argumentative woman of a few minutes ago. He swallowed hard. "How was she killed?"

Flora looked past Joe. "That flag. That flag killed her. That's why I'm going to stamp on it."

"Bullshit!" Smith said. "You can't blame everything on us. We don't do everything that's wrong with the world."

"As sure as I'm breathing, that flag killed her."

"Kick 'er, Joe. Boot 'er right out the door."

"I used to march all over the South. Used to sit in at lunch counters."

"You ain't did nothing. Kick 'er, Joe."

"You don't know her, do you Tyroll?" Joe asked.

Tyroll wiped his face with his palm.

"He don't know you. Never heard of you. You just another one of these crazies come in from Milledgeville. Crazy as a loon in June. Kick 'er out, Joe."

Flora felt Tyroll studying her. She threw back her head, trying to appear confident, but she could not look at him. She looked at the flag, then glanced across the room to the couple in the booth who were locked in embrace.

"Flora Devine." She tossed her name out carelessly, not thinking to aim it at Tyroll. "Flora Devine. I marched in Selma." She thought to berate Tyroll. What did he know? He was just a drunk. "I marched in Selma."

"You marched to the toilet," Smith said. "To the goddamn toilet 'n' back."

Tyroll cleared his throat. "I reckon I know her," he said slowly. "I reckon I do."

"Who is she then?" Smith pressed.

"I seen her on the TV."

"Who is she then?"

Tyroll looked uneasy. "She who she say she is." He ran his palm over his face and let his head slump.

"Flora Devine." She lifted her head. "Thank you, sir." She turned to Joe and Smith. "You see who I am."

"I'm sorry, ma'am," Joe said.

"Shit!" Smith said.

"Be respectable," Joe warned him.

"Yes," Flora said. "You all should be respectable and take down that flag. Change the name of this place."

"I can't do that," Joe said. "I'm not the owner, and besides, the customers like it."

"I'm a customer," Flora said. Her energy was waning. "He's a customer." She pointed to Tyroll.

"I'm a customer, too," Smith said.

Her nerve was going. The sadness was beginning to creep up on her. "Here." She shoved the twenty at Joe. "Take my money."

"Oh, no, ma'am. It's on the house."

"Don't insult me. I can pay."

Joe took the money and went to get the change.

Flora was standing, steadying herself against the bar. She moved a step toward Smith and stopped. He was drinking a Schlitz from the can.

His face was haggard and grizzly with white stubs of beard. "Now take my friend, Tyroll, over there," he said, his roan teeth showing. "Tyroll 'n' me been knowing each other since we were boys—'n' we always got along. You just got to know where you are wanted."

Flora stepped the other way toward Tyroll. His chin was slumped on his chest. He looked asleep, but his hand rubbed the bald spot on his head. Taking her hand from the counter only long enough to get around Tyroll, Flora unsteadily walked toward the flag. The X, the bars, were taller than a man. It was a Confederate soldier or one of Bull Connor's policemen with raised billy club. The rest of the barroom was a blur as she tunneled down the length of the counter toward the flag.

"Wouldn't do that if I were you, ma'am," Joe said.

She heard him but reached out for the flag and twisted the corner of it into her fist. The fabric was old and soft and her fingers easily punched through it.

"Don't do that!" Joe shouted. "I told you I'm not the owner."

Flora increased the tension on the flag, pulling it away from the wall. A rip began on one side about halfway up the X. "I'm gone get that man in there. You see him? I'm gone cut him in half before he gets to me."

▼ ▼ ▼

After the divorce, she and Priscilla moved into an apartment complex located along a busy highway. The children who lived in the complex often took a shortcut across the highway in order to get to school.

One day when Flora came home from teaching, a policeman stopped her outside the apartment door. "Are you Mrs. Devine?" he asked. He was sandy-haired and baby-faced, too young to be a policeman, she thought. "I'm sorry to inform you," he said. "There has been an accident. It was bound to happen. It could have happened to anyone."

Flora remained calm. She kept thinking about what a lovely day it was. How the big, white clouds were rolling across the sky. She went to the morgue to identify Priscilla's jewelry. They wouldn't let her see the body. The truck driver who had hit Priscilla was waiting outside the morgue. He was a stout, grizzled white man. He had been crying. He took Flora's hand. "I swear, I didn't see her. I didn't see her," he said. Flora accepted his apology. She walked in a circle. "Can I take you home?" he asked. She declined. He sat her on a bench outside the morgue.

"Is that the truck?" she asked. It was a semi. On the grill was painted a Confederate flag.

▼ ▼ ▼

"Crazy bitch," Smith shouted. "Do that 'n' I'm fixin' to kick yo' black ass out of here myself." Flora pulled again. Dust flew up and the rip made its way to the waist of the X but did not cut it.

Joe had come through the gate in the counter. He walked slowly with both palms out. "Ma'am, I don't want to call the police. I can appreciate what you want, but there's nothing I can do about it. What's past is past. We have got to think about the future."

"I just want to get that man!"

"This is not the way to do it. This will only cause trouble."

"Ain' no trouble for me." Flora jerked. A long ripping sound knifed the room. Except for Tyroll, the customers were looking at Flora and the flag, but no one, not even Smith, moved.

▼ ▼ ▼

The night was moonless and a fog had settled along Ponce de Leon Avenue. Flora only vaguely knew where she was. She lived in Westend and she needed to find a bus stop. She walked through two boarded-up blocks, and in the third, near a pawnshop, she saw the bus stop next to a telephone pole. She steadied herself against the pole. About her, in the fog, the streetlights glowed in eerie yellow spheres. A car passed. She closed her eyes. She heard nothing.

Suddenly an arm was around her neck. She could not scream. She was dragged into the darkness of a back alley. Her heels drummed across the asphalt. She clawed at the forearms, digging her fingertips into the sinew. Her ears were ringing. Her head was swelling from lack of breath. She flailed. She tasted the sweaty, hairy forearm. Her heels made music on the pavement. She was dropped on her back. She gasped. The air rushed in, hurting her throat.

She could not see the man, but she knew he stood over her. Suddenly his face glowed in the flare of a match as he lit a cigarette. She struggled to stand, but the man pushed her down and sat on her knees. He put the blade of a hunting knife to her throat.

"Do you know who I am?" he whispered. "Do you know who I am?" She did not answer. "Do you know who I am?" Ashes from the cigarette fell on her chest and burned her. The knife punctured the skin under her neck. "Answer me," he pleaded. "Do you know who I am?"

"Yes. You're Mr. Dixie."

He took the blade from her throat and held it arm's length above his head. "I'm Mr. Death," he said. "Just Death to you."

She heard the first thud as the blade struck her chest, and she heard the dozen that followed, but they seemed to become fainter and fainter as if coming from a greater and greater distance. After awhile, the man went away.

Quiet followed, but she was not afraid. Then there were lights and voices. She heard someone ask, "Who is she? Do you know who she is?"

"Flora Devine," she thought. "Flora Devine."

# Jack 'n' Jill

▼
▼
▼

Every Friday afternoon George Cox and his wife Louise went shopping in town. They put their two children, Calvin and Candace, in the huge backseat of the 1960 Oldsmobile; not a new car, but new to them. The car was black and had tail fins, and the children called it the Batmobile after a car in a TV show.

For George, Friday was a day of anticipation. On the one hand, he anticipated his paycheck from Mr. Phillips at Phillips' Garage. The paycheck always disappointed him. No matter how hard he worked, it seemed never to grow beyond eighty dollars a week. Out of that he paid for food, clothes, mortgage, and whatever else they needed. Louise's pay from day work was fifteen dollars. She had three days, three different families to clean for. They had a little egg money, too. When the hens were laying well, George and Louise could expect ten or twelve dozen eggs—they would give away a dozen or two to the sick and shut-in—and sell the others to Henson's Store for an extra dollar. They managed.

On the other hand, George looked forward to the trip to town. It was like a short vacation. He imagined it to be like the ones he had seen in advertisements for cars in magazines. Happy white families were taking car trips. The rose-cheeked children looked with awe from the car windows at the Grand Canyon or Niagara Falls. The stylish wife carried a wicker picnic basket from which a checkered cloth protruded. The father, always handsome and slim, dressed in a fedora and sport coat and drove the Chevrolet or Ford. In these pictures, the father had an air of confidence, and George imagined how the children must have adored the father for the delight he brought to their lives.

The town of Jeffersonville was about half an hour away on U.S. 250. The road wound through the piedmont and at times seesawed over the hills. The children enjoyed it when George let the car pick up speed and swoop into the valleys so that the inertia made their stomachs turn over. Louise protested that it was dangerous. Besides, Billy Cooper, the state policeman who patrolled the area, might stop him. No colored person wanted to be stopped by Billy Cooper. But when the children laughed so heartily at the ticklish feeling in their bellies, George and Louise looked at each other and laughed, too. The last hill before the town was called Little Mountain. George downshifted the car to get to the top. As the car strained up the hill, he teased the children that it was the little engine that could. At the crest of the hill, they could see the town spread out below them, with its central business district and little white and yellow houses on the quiet streets where white families lived.

The shopping had its own brief routine. First, Louise went into Leggett's Department Store where the colored were treated well enough. She made a payment on the layaway and, as needed, bought clothing or school supplies for the children. George walked the children to the colored park, where they played on the slides and swings. They already had a rope swing at home that George had hung from an oak's limb, so the children mostly played on the slide. After the playground, they would meet Louise at the car and go grocery shopping at Kroger's. Here they went in as a family. Everybody had a job. George pushed the cart. Louise read the list. Calvin helped Louise find and gather the items. Candace, just four, sat in the child's seat of the cart and charmed the other shoppers. They formed a tight pack as they went down the aisle. George was especially proud that his children were quiet and obedient. On more than one occasion he had observed some white child having a tantrum, crying about some item he or she wanted. His children never did this, nor were they dirty or snotty, like some colored children. When Calvin wasn't helping his mother, he walked at George's side, holding onto his trouser legs or to the side of the cart. As a special treat, they always stopped at Jack 'n' Jill's afterward for a custard cone.

Jack 'n' Jill's was just on the way out of town. It had a swooped roof, like a sliding board, Calvin said. The roof was outlined in red neon, and on top, outlined in bulbs, were the figures of a freckled redheaded boy with a gigantic cowlick and his sister with yellow pigtails. They flashed off and on, casting a red tint on the parking lot even though the sun was still up. The restaurant had large windows on the front, through which they could see the grill cooks in their white caps and aprons.

"Jack and Jill," the children called as George parked.

"Yes," Louise encouraged, and they all recited. "Jack and Jill went up the hill to fetch a pail of water. Jack fell down and broke his crown, and Jill came tumbling after."

"But he doesn't have a crown," Calvin insisted.

"Crown means head," his mother said.

"If you use your head," George said and patted his own head, "it's like wearing a crown."

Two lines had formed in front of the restaurant. George took his place in the colored line. Long ago, the sign that said "Colored" had been taken down, but still people knew which line was which. In the larger cities, such distinctions were breaking down, but in Jeffersonville they remained. He nodded to the man and woman in front of him. He didn't know them, but they seemed to be people like himself, country folks who had come into town for their weekly shopping. Their lives had a peaceful regularity, broken only now and again by some violent interruption. Even these interruptions could mostly be avoided, if people played smart and did what was expected of them.

A half-dozen teenagers, boys and girls on a date, were in the other line. The boys wore cuffed jeans and penny loafers, and the girls had on plaid skirts and wore bows in their hair. In contrast to the sober colored line, this line was boisterous. The boys teased each other, and the girls talked giddily back and forth. From what George could gather, they were on their way to a football game at the white high school.

A tractor trailer drove up and parked along the highway. Truckers often stopped here, and George paid no particular attention until he saw that this trucker was a colored man. He was slightly older than George, about thirty, with closely cut hair and a prominent bald spot. As he approached the line, he nodded at George, and George nodded back. He prepared himself to have a conversation with the trucker. It was not often that a colored trucker passed through these parts.

But the trucker didn't get in line with George. Instead, he pushed through the crowd of teens and headed for the front door. For a moment the teens stopped talking. They moved out of the trucker's way. One girl made a face.

He must have a delivery, George thought, and turned to face the front of the restaurant. The teenagers were ordering now, and when they were done the cashier would start to take orders in the colored line again. Suddenly one of the white girls gasped. George looked up and saw that the teenagers were staring through the restaurant window at the trucker, who had seated himself at the counter and had picked up a menu. For just a moment, George wondered if Jack 'n' Jill had started serving colored people inside. He hadn't heard that they were or that any white lunch counter in Jeffersonville was. He glanced at the tags on the truck. New Jersey. The trucker was a stranger. George's face flushed. He should have known when the trucker first approached. There were no colored truckers from around here. Trucking paid too well for that.

Besides, a colored trucker couldn't go all the places that truckers needed to go. He should have known the moment the man got out of his truck. He should have known that a trucker wouldn't make a delivery to the front. He should have stopped him before he went inside and told him where the colored people stood to get served. George wondered if there was a way to let the trucker know.

The heavyset woman in front of George turned to him with a worried look. "You reckon he gonna start up something?"

George shook his head. "I figure he just don't know no better."

The woman smoothed the sides of her face. "I reckon they gonna let him know."

The words had hardly left her mouth when they saw the counterman approach the trucker. He spoke to him in what seemed a mannerly way and then stood back expectantly. The trucker did not move; instead, he appeared to be placing an order. Again the clerk spoke, seemingly to reason with the trucker. Again, the trucker held out the menu and pointed to items.

"Lawd," the big woman said. "I reckon he must be gonna cause trouble. Now why don't he just act right?" She grinned, and her eyes shifted worriedly. "I just want me a foot-long."

The man in front of the woman turned and agreed with her. He just wanted a bag of onion rings and a double-large vanilla. There was something about the way onion and ice cream tasted when you ate them together. George wanted to laugh, but he turned to face the car. He could see Louise through the windshield. The upper half of her face was obscured behind the tinted part of the windshield, so that her serene face seemed divided. She was sitting patiently, as if dreaming. Then she turned to look into the backseat, as if to speak to one of the children. Candace's braided head poked over the seat. He could not see Calvin. He made up his mind that if the police came, he would leave right away. He would not put his children in danger. A few years before, four little girls had been blown up in Birmingham, and just that summer, children had been hurt in the Watts riots. He was glad he lived in the country, where life was slow and predictable. In the city, even in a midsize town like Jeffersonville, things could go out of control at any moment.

The trucker just sat. Two of the cooks stood looking at him. A couple who had been sitting near the middle of the counter when he came in had moved to the far side, allowing plenty of room between themselves and the trucker. The teenagers continued to order, and the cook at their window began to fill the orders. The interruption seemed to be over, and the restaurant started to go on as before, operating around the obstacle of the trucker.

Maybe they should just go ahead and serve the man, George thought. After all, he wasn't from around here, and he didn't know any better. The local colored people still wouldn't eat inside. It just wasn't something they would do.

The man in front of George got his onion rings and double-large cone. He had a look of relief on his face. As he passed George, his tongue curled around the top of the swirl of soft ice cream and scooped it into his mouth. Cream oozed out of the corners of his mouth, and his eyes lit up.

What was he so happy about? George thought. The ice cream was good, but it wasn't that good. Maybe the man was gloating, relieved that he had been served and was getting away without incident.

Before the big woman ahead of George ordered, the clerk waited on a middle-aged white couple. The man was dressed in tweeds and a hat; the woman wore a long wool coat and leather gloves. He must be a doctor or a lawyer, George thought. He listened as they discussed with the clerk how they wanted their burgers garnished. Suddenly the man stopped in midsentence, and George knew that he had seen the trucker. When the white man continued, he sounded nervous. His wife interrupted him. "What kind of a place is this? We had better go." The cook insisted that the burgers would only take a few minutes, but the couple turned away. As they turned, the man looked squarely at George. At first, George admired the blankness of the man's face. Well-off white folks, he thought, could always mask so well how they were feeling. Though they walked briskly, they exuded an aloof dignity. The man opened the door for the woman; the woman folded the tail of her coat behind her as she got into the car; the car itself was polished, new, a Cadillac.

George thought that he would like to have such presence. It would be nice to have a new Cadillac, too, instead of the secondhand Oldsmobile; but more than the car, he longed to have a presence. The man walked as if he had not a care in the world, as if he expected other people to move out of his way, to give him and his wife space as they walked to the car. Even the way the man lifted off his fedora as he got into his car and pulled the door shut, rather than slamming it, suggested he had presence.

George's attention turned to the big woman in front of him. "Foo'long," she said. She was breathless. "Foo'long, foo'long." The cook questioned her about the relishes she wanted, and the excited woman ordered, changed her mind, ordered again. Her body swayed, as if she couldn't stand still anticipating her foot-long. George looked back at the trucker, whose attention was focused on the colored line. Slowly, the trucker's face took on a look of disdain, and George realized that the look he had seen on the white man's face was not just blankness but disdain as well. Suddenly, he felt a part of a triangle. One point was the dignified white couple; the second the trucker; and the third was the foolish fat woman, who was blathering out her order. George felt in the middle, and he didn't know which way to turn.

The trucker folded the menu and stood.

"Oh, Jesus," the heavy woman said. "He ain't..." she started to walk away, but the cook called out her order, and she waddled back and paid for it.

The trucker walked slowly to the door and then outside. He was not as tall as he looked sitting at the stool, not as big as truckers sometimes are. He had a tense body and moved like a soldier. He walked straight toward George, and George thought he would now get in the colored line. He was relieved, but disappointed, too. Then the trucker stopped just short of George and made a crushing movement with the toe of his shoe. George heard the gravel grind beneath the trucker's shoe and saw both anger and disgust in his face. Not a word had been spoken, but what the trucker had meant made George sick to his stomach.

"Next," the cook called, and the word rang in George's ear. He looked at the trucker who was climbing the ladder into his cab. He looked at his family. The children had tumbled into the front seat, and their innocent faces looked toward him expectantly. "Next," the cook said impatiently. "What do you want?"

▼ ▼ ▼

George drove down Little Mountain, out of the city and into the rolling countryside. The trees were mostly brown, with only a tinge of rust left in the oaks. The poplars and maples were already skeletons. All this went by in a blur: the trees, the blonde fields, and the spotted cattle. Large farms, former plantations, seemed to dance in the distance as the car roller-coastered down the road. Country stores with their bubble-topped gas pumps and weatherworn houses with front porches cluttered with flowerpots swayed by the car. The car seemed not to move, but rather the road seemed to move under it.

"George," Louise called to him, her voice high with concern. "Aren't you going to eat your cone?" George looked at his fist, which gripped the cone. The peak of the swirl had lain down, and the sides had turned glossy. Trickles of cream ran over his thumb and down the ridges of his fingers. He could feel the crispness of the cone give away in spots. He put the cone to his lips, but as he did so, what he feared would happen happened. His stomach hardened. It would not accept the treat. In his mind he saw the face of the trucker, the corners of his lips turned down and his eyes widening as if to ask, "Ain't you folks got any pride?"

Calvin poked his head over the backseat. His eyes were lit with glee, and his breath was sweet with ice cream. "Daddy, I'll eat it if you don't want to."

"Sit down," his mother ordered. She offered to take the cone and to divide it among herself and the children. Already her cone was half eaten. George looked in the mirror at his children. Candace's little tongue had poked holes in the side of her ice cream, and she had made mouse bites around the ridges of the cone. All that was left of Calvin's cone was a milk mustache. He looked at Candace's cone—greedily, George thought. He resisted a sudden urge to slap his son.

Louise dabbed at his hand with a napkin. "For Pete's sake, George, either eat it or give it to us. Don't waste it."

"Yeah, Daddy," Calvin added, "eat it or give it to me."

"Shut up," George said and quickly amended, "I mean be quiet, please." But he had meant "shut up." He did not want to see his child groveling for the ice cream. Any other time he might have laughed, but he still stung from the disdain he had seen on the face of the truck driver and the grinding of his shoe in the gravel. The trucker had walked so straight and tall and then had stopped just in front of him and ground his shoe the way he might crush a roach, only more intensely. The trucker couldn't have done that to the man in the fedora, and not just because the man was white and well-to-do but because he had a presence.

Louise stopped dabbing at the ice cream that was now making a pool next to George's lap. The cone was mushy, and it was beginning to feel as if he were holding oatmeal. "What's wrong?" Louise whispered. "What happened?" Her voice was so lovely, he slowed the car. He wanted to hear it again, above the groan of the engine. He looked her squarely in the face. Her face was an almond, a thing of such natural beauty as to be wondrous. The almond flower was delicate and fragrant. He had seen the trees flowering in the yards of the rich folks in town. The shell was perfectly shaped and golden when the sun hit it at a certain slant. The kernel was not just sweet but meaty. "You're a nut," he said.

She shook her head and chuckled with incredulity. "*You're* the nut."

"I'll tell you what I mean later," he said. With that, he tossed the ice cream out the window. "Don't look back," he said to Calvin, who had turned to look out the back window.

They rode in silence for a moment, and then Louise began to furiously wipe at the seat. "What in the world got into you, is what I want to know? If you didn't want that cone, you shouldn't have bought it."

"There are some things a man can't eat," George answered her softly. It seemed to him that she was two people. There was the scolding Louise, who was drifting farther and farther away, a head mouthing unintelligible sounds, and there was the almond-faced Louise, who seemed to grow more golden brown as the sun glanced the treetops and the shadows grew long. His own voice, too, seemed distant to him. He wasn't angry, not even concerned with the scolding, because he knew Louise would understand once he had a chance to explain. Some things a man of heart just could not eat. Would the man in tweed have eaten that cone? Would the trucker? He imagined at that moment the cool swagger of Jackie Robinson stepping up to bat. Jackie leaned over home plate, elbows up, bat high. He waved the bat in a little circle, adjusted his grip, and faced the pitcher. Brooklyn never had it so good. Jackie never would have eaten that cone, never would have stood in line for it.

"It's not like money was growing on trees," Louise was saying. "Leastways not a tree I've ever seen."

"You're right, honey. But you pay for things in more ways than just with money."

"Well, I'd *like* to get ahold of one of those ways."

George smiled. They had come to the series of hills that the children liked. He sped up to give the car good momentum as it crested the first hill.

"Here we go," called Calvin, and Candace repeated, "Here we go again."

"George!" Louise turned her face to the window. "Set a decent example for the children."

"The children…," George said, as they swooped into the bottom.

"Owwwww," Candace hollered. "That one *almost* hurt." She and Calvin laughed. George chuckled and turned to Louise. She still had her face to the window, and when she faced him, he couldn't quite read her expression. It was both bemused and alarmed. "There's a cop." Then her face hardened, which meant "I told you so."

George looked in the rearview mirror and slowed the car. He looked where he thought the cop must be hiding, and saw nothing. For a long moment his stomach still floated. Everything around him seemed tense and aslant. He had begun to crest the second hill. Perhaps if he made it that far and saw nothing behind him, he would get away. Just as the top of the hill came up behind him, he looked in the mirror and saw the police car pull onto the highway. Hope began to drain. All he could do was to drive along reasonably and wish the policeman would pass him. The police car rode behind him for awhile, gradually catching up to him. Then, as if the cop had grown tired of teasing him, the red lights flashed on. Louise's eyes were round with excitement, but her voice was quiet. "Oh, God. It's Billy Cooper."

George got out of the car and walked back to meet Billy Cooper.

Though a handsome man, Billy Cooper did not cut an impressive figure. His shirt seemed too large for him and his pants too short. Around his waist he wore a large gun belt loaded with his police equipment: a flashlight, a gun, handcuffs and a club. George reminded himself that he had to be careful about the club. It was rumored that Cooper had killed with it.

"You were speedin'," the officer said. "I got you doing eighty coming down that hill."

"Yes, suh," said George. He avoided looking directly at Billy Cooper, thinking that he might get off if he played the part just right. He was aware that behind him his children were sneaking glances out the back window, despite his stern warning to them to keep their eyes forward. Thank God they couldn't hear him. If he held his body just right, it would appear to them that he was standing straight and carrying on a conversation with the policeman. If he kept his eyes low and didn't look at the children, only the policeman would see the deference.

"Where you going to in such a hurry, boy?"

"Going home."

"Where you coming from?"

"Shopping."

"You go all the way to Jeffersonville to buy your groceries? You too good to buy your food at a country store?"

"No, suh." George shuffled his feet nervously, then reflexively glanced at the car. Only Candace was looking.

"Where you live?—Give me your license." Cooper studied the license for a moment. "Cox? You that boy works at Phillips' Garage?"

"Yes, suh."

"I seen you there."

"Yes, suh."

"Mr. Phillips is a right good ole boy. He give me free tune-ups and such."

"Yes, suh."

"Well, now. 'Cause you work for Mr. Phillips, I'm gonna let you go this time. I don't reckon Mr. Phillips need one of his boys losing a day going over to the courthouse for speeding."

"No, suh." George exaggerated his relief with a sigh. He didn't care what Mr. Phillips needed. It was he that didn't need the expense of a traffic ticket.

Cooper gave the license back and pulled his belt up. He chuckled and leaned against the fender of the police car. "You know, I give something a ticket I ain't never give a ticket to before."

"Yes, suh," George said in a more relaxed tone. The threat was over; Cooper just wanted to chat now.

"Yessirree. I bet you ain't never seen one of these either, not in these parts. Even working for old man Phillips, I bet you never heard of a *nigger* truck driver."

George's eyes fixed on Cooper's steel-toed shoes. They were caked with mud, even though it hadn't rained in several days. George's mouth was dry and his stomach hard. He tried to hold a pleasant smile on his face.

"I don't mean no bread truck or milk truck. I know you see a couple of them in Richmond. I mean a for-real eighteen-wheeler, *interstate* rig. A Mack. A great big sucker. Got to climb up a ladder to get in the cab. Thing must have eight or ten gears in it. You never thought a *nigger* could drive one of those."

George looked up and saw Billy Cooper throw his head back and laugh. His teeth were crooked and stained, and strands of hair stuck out from his nostrils. "A nigger driving a truck like that."

To the children, George thought, it must seem that he and Officer Cooper were having a laugh. Perhaps they would think their father had told a joke that was so funny the officer went into a fit of laughing. Then a curious thought entered George's head. What would the truck driver think? The truck driver who was nowhere around? Somehow, he would know that George was shuffling his feet and grinning while this stupid white man laughed at the thought of a colored man driving a truck.

At this point, he should have said, “No, suh. I have never seen anything like that. Not in my wildest dreams.” Then he could have gone to his car and driven home. But he kept staring at Cooper’s twisted, laughing face.

Cooper stopped laughing. “What’s wrong, boy?”

“Nothing,” George said.

Cooper adjusted his belt and put his hand on the club. “You ain’t answered my question. You ever seen a nigger rigdriver?”

George looked into the distance at the long shadows of hay rolls on the harvested fields. He looked at the clouds stretching out along the horizon. The sun was setting. He looked at Cooper’s hand on his club. He glanced back at the car. Both children were watching. Louise was watching. He knew that somewhere, beyond the darkening hills, the trucker was watching, too.

# Old Lee Brown

As he had done every day for fifty years, old Lee Brown sat by the window of the Corner Market and looked out on Howard Square. Before desegregation, Howard Square had been a neat, industrious neighborhood comprised of about one hundred and fifty houses. Many of its residents were country folks who had moved their families to Atlanta in order to work for the railroads or in the textile mills. Women who didn't work the mills rode the trolleys to white neighborhoods to do day work.

On their way home from work, people slipped into the Corner Market to buy beans, rice, sugar, flour, or coffee and to chat with Lee Brown. In his produce section he offered them potatoes and yams and, when they were in season, squash, English peas, snap beans, and collards. In the meat box he kept sausages, bacon, fatback, ham hocks, eggs, and chicken. During the holiday season he sold fresh turkey, chitterlings, and beef.

More than any of his neighbors, Lee Brown was known as a man who loved Howard Square. He seemed to know everyone by name—even the children. He knew what each person did for a living, and took pride in their accomplishments. Though neither a religious man nor a politician, he went regularly to all the churches: Baptist, AME, and Holiness. In all of them he was nicknamed the Youth Deacon because of his enthusiasm for children's accomplishments. Whether the child had won a scholarship, had been accepted to a college, or merely had a good report card, he made a point of recognizing and praising the child before the congregation.

He helped the parents, too, because to help parents helped the children. Children would succeed if they were well sheltered and well fed. When parents were having trouble financing their homes, he co-signed loans. When his neighbors needed to make additions or repairs to their homes, he came with hammer and saw. When someone was out of work and needed food, he carried them on his ledger. People knew that the few cents more they paid for goods at the Corner Market went to help less fortunate neighbors. They also knew that if they fell on hard times, Lee Brown would help them in any way possible.

He took pride in walking down the streets of cottages and hipped-roof bungalows. He looked for signs that his neighbors were prospering—a newly painted fence, a garden in season—and delighted in finding them. But he took greater delight in knowing that he had played a part in improving the lives of his neighbors.

Twenty-five years after desegregation, the houses Lee Brown had taken such pride in were abandoned. Many of them were boarded up, their yards left to grow wild. Some had burned, and their charred timbers were draped with thickets of kudzu. Others had simply rotted: once-straight roofs had become swaybacked. Alcoholics and addicts squatted in them.

All around Howard Square, the city had continued to grow. Through his window, Lee Brown could see downtown's glistening stone and glass skyscrapers. Overhead planes circled as they approached the international airport. If he concentrated, Lee Brown could hear the constant hum of the twelve-lane highway a few blocks away. The freight yards and the textile mills were long gone.

Howard Square was worse than a ghost town, Lee Brown thought. In a ghost town there were no people, not even ghosts; but in Howard Square people remained. Most were old. Where young men once wooed young women or preened in their vested suits before their automobiles, now the old hobbled on three-pronged canes or sat lonely on their porches. Where many children once played hopscotch, hula hoop and marbles, now only a few idled. They were ragged, snotty, and smart-mouthed. Children once thought of him as a kindly uncle; now they eyed him with suspicion. Rarely would they take candy from his hand, although they often stole it behind his back. Still, Lee Brown loved the children and tried to make friends with them when he could.

▼ ▼ ▼

Two boys came into the store. He knew one of the boys was Precious Davis' grandson, a boy he had tried to befriend on several occasions. The other he had never seen.

"How's your grandma?" he asked and turned off the radio so he could hear.

The boy was about fifteen, long-limbed, with a small round head and a cap of tight naps that made his head look like an acorn. He shrugged nervously and mumbled. When he smiled, his eyes shifted to the other boy, and Mr. Brown got an uneasy feeling that the smile was fake.

The other boy seemed older, but not much. He was a plump yellow boy with an empty look in his eye. His hands were shoved into his pockets. Mr. Brown nodded to him and came to the cash register. On a shelf under the register he kept a small pistol. Just the rumor that he had one was enough to frighten most neighborhood boys. He had pulled it twice since the integration, just to let some ruffians see he meant business when he asked them to leave the premises. Fifty years ago, it was enough just to tell a boy, "I'm going to tell your momma."

"What can I get for you, son?" he asked Precious' grandson.

"Just the money," the strange boy answered.

Mr. Brown wanted to laugh, the request was made so matter-of-factly. He felt for his gun, but his fingers were clumsy and they brushed the gun, pushing it further under the shelf. Now, to reach it he would have to bend down and look for it. All of this seemed to happen in a bemused slowness; while Lee was concerned with the gun, the boy had taken a gun of his own from his pocket and was aiming it at him. Looking at the small black barrel pointed at him made Lee Brown suddenly dizzy. Even though he had been to war, he had never had a gun pointed at him. The boy reached across the narrow counter, poked the gun into his ribs and twisted it back and forth.

"Don't bug out on me, Grandpa. Just give me what you got in the register."

"There's just a little," Lee Brown's voice quavered slightly. "Now you be calm, son. I'll give it to you. Don't get jumpy." He said this, all the time remarking to himself how calmly he was speaking and how he would tell Gloria about it when he got home. She would be worried for days, of course…and then he remembered that his wife had been dead for five years. Remembering Gloria's death shook his confidence more than the gun.

The register drawer sprang open, and the strange boy instructed Precious' grandson to take out the money. "Fuck the pennies. Get the paper." Because they left the coins, they took less than fifty dollars, one day's bank. They were the first customers that day. Then the strange boy asked for Lee Brown's wallet.

"I ain't got a thing in it."

"I ain't asked what was in it." The boy pulled the old wallet apart. Out fell Mr. Brown's identification card, what the state gives you to replace your license when you are too old to drive. Out fell his NAACP membership card, his Medicare card. Out fell a picture of his grandson as a baby, his daughter from New York with one of her husbands, a black-and-white of his wife taken at the state fair grounds in the 1940s.

"Credit cards," the boy demanded.

"Don't believe in them."

"You believe in this?" The boy put the gun up to Mr. Brown's forehead.

Slowly Lee Brown spoke, "Son, I have given you what I have."

"And I'll give you a bullet right in your goddamn head," the boy said. His eyes had a hollow look to them. It was almost as if they were glass eyes. But then he smirked incongruously. Lee Brown couldn't make up his mind how serious the predicament was. Was this only a stickup, and the boy only trying to frighten him, or was murder part of the plan? A shiver ran through him. He reasoned that if it were a killing the boy wanted, he would have killed already. The boy took the gun from Lee Brown's forehead and looked around the store. "You ain't got shit in here."

Lee Brown looked at Precious' boy out of the corner of his eye and realized that he had already made a fatal mistake. He had asked the boy about his grandmother. He could identify the boy.

▼ ▼ ▼

Just last evening he had spoken to Precious Davis. Many years ago Precious had suffered a stroke and now spent most of the day sitting in a rocking chair. She still had good sense and could talk a blue streak. Lee Brown had pulled himself up the stairs to her porch and had sat with her. As he often did, he began telling her about the successes of his children. Sometimes he forgot what he had and hadn't told her, but he enjoyed talking about his children. Elena, his middle daughter, had tenure at the university. "That means they can't fire her. She'll make good money for life." Harry, the youngest, was a vice president at his corporation. There were several vice presidents, but Harry was the only black one. Harry's son Todd had been accepted to Harvard. "We've come a long way," he summarized.

Throughout his rambling Precious had seemed agitated, a bit nervous. "Todd?" she said. "I never could get used to that name."

"How's your grandboy?" Lee Brown asked. "He giving you any trouble?"

She adjusted her sweater and made two short rocks in her chair. "Trouble no more," she quipped. She asked about Silvie, Lee Brown's oldest daughter. Precious had been a friend of Gloria's and knew the family well. She always asked about Silvie. On the surface she was just being polite—just asking about everybody—but Lee Brown wondered if this might be her way of poking at him for his bragging. Precious had not had the same good fortune with her family as he'd had with his. Her eldest son had been killed in Vietnam. The younger son was in prison for selling drugs. Her grandson was the son of the younger. He sometimes lived with Precious and sometimes with his mother. Though she would not admit it now, not after all of Lee Brown's bragging, she had said once that he was hard to handle.

"Oh, Silvie…" Lee Brown wondered if he should lie and say Silvie was doing well. The truth was he hadn't heard from Silvie for about six months. The other two children visited weekly. Elena came on Wednesdays to make sure the house was clean and that he had food and medicine. Harry came on the weekends to do chores. He brought along Todd to help. Silvie lived in New York and visited only once a year.

When she came she put on like she was queen of the Ritz. She wore clothes more suited to her nightclub act, and she smoked thin brown cigarettes with no filters. The last time she came home, at Christmas, Elena had brought her by the store to surprise him.

"Daddy, Daddy, Daddy." Silvie had glanced around the store and had looked at him with a touch of sadness in her eyes. "Why do you insist on keeping this place open?" She rubbed a fleck of tobacco off her front teeth. "No one comes in here unless it's to buy cigarettes or Coca Cola." She turned to Elena and then to the empty store as if an audience were there. "Why, darling, they have vending machines to do that!"

"Call me a vending machine then," Lee Brown answered her sternly. "Even a damn machine needs something to do."

He could never stay angry with Silvie. More than the others, she looked like his wife. She had an oval face with a broad nose, thick lips and a curved-down mouth. Her cheekbones were as high as an Indian's, and her eyes were round with long lashes. Her skin was clear and brown, like black tea. She had ample and shapely flesh on a small frame and a daring grace in the way she moved. She was so fluid that when she gestured, he could follow the movement from her shoulder all the way to her fingertips.

Precious interrupted his daydream about Silvie. "With all the effort I put into them, I wonder if it was worth it."

"Of course, Mrs. Davis, it was worth it." Lee Brown stamped his foot. How could Precious even think otherwise?

"Sometimes I don't know. I look around at the neighborhood and see it looking so bad. Everybody moved away except us old folks. And the ones that ain't old, you can't shake a stick at. What would it have been like, Mr. Brown, if we hadn't worked so hard to make it so good?"

Her question gnawed at him. Howard Square seemed to have fallen apart gradually, slowly depleted of the people who should have been its life's blood. In a way he had celebrated each small depletion, each time a child won a scholarship to a faraway college or gotten a good job outside the neighborhood. "When I was young," he said, not clearly knowing what he meant, "I did my part."

"You sure did, Lee." She used his first name for emphasis. "But was any of it worth it?"

▼ ▼ ▼

The boy with the gun caught him by the wrist. "What's that on your hand?"

"My wedding band."

"Give it here."

Lee Brown tried to loosen his wrist. "Ain't worth nothing."

"Give it here." The boy let go of Lee Brown's wrist and pushed the gun against his chest.

Lee Brown thought about knocking away the gun. If I were younger, he thought, just ten years younger. The boy, though plump, was solid, and he held his finger on the trigger. Lee Brown could smell both the clean machine oil and the boy's sour hand.

Slowly, Lee Brown pulled the ring off his finger and laid it on the counter. "I have worn that ring for fifty-seven years." Would the boy care? Did anybody care? "First, I wore it on my left hand." He placed his left hand on the counter for the boys to see. "After my wife died I moved it to my right hand. To my death finger." Until death do you part, he thought. That was true, and it wasn't true. Death takes away the person, but the memories remain. Slowly and surely, if you outlived someone by long enough, someone you cared to remember, you would live your life over with them many times.

"It's turned green," the fat boy said and tossed the ring over his shoulder.

"Come on," Precious' grandson said. "Let's get the hell out of here."

Lee Brown took a deep breath and held it. The plump boy moved toward the door, backing out like he was an actor in a gangster movie. Lee thought about the gun under the shelf, but common sense told him to stay put. "You're too slow to act a fool," he thought.

Then the plump boy stopped. "Naw," he said. "He know us. He a talker." Lee Brown took a short breath. "I can see it in his eye. He a talker. He know you."

"He don't know me," Precious' grandson said. "Let him go. He just an old man. He probably ain't got sense to talk."

Lee Brown tried to agree with Precious' boy. "I'm just an old man. Old Lee Brown. Ain't got good sense, sitting up babysitting a store all day long. Just play storekeeping. Just keeping busy. Not like this store means anything to me. I wouldn't say a word to the police. Hell, the police wouldn't believe a crazy old fool like me anyway. I'm crazy, see. Just a crazy fool..." When he realized he was mumbling, Lee Brown flushed. He could feel his face burn, and he knew that it was red. But he began to hope. Maybe they would think he was getting sick—a heart attack. He could fall over on the counter. This thought made him flush even more. He had been a soldier in the United States Army, and a marcher for civil rights, but now he was so afraid he would fake a heart attack.

"What's the matter with him?" the plump boy asked. "He choking?"

"He sick. See? Let's go. He sick."

The plump boy stepped forward with the gun pointed at Lee Brown. "He sick? I put him down. He won't know the difference. Be a favor to him."

"Naw, he be dead 'fore we get around the corner. Let him be."

With the gun pointing at him again, the calm floating feeling came back to Lee Brown. He gained control of his breathing. He could see that this boy wanted to kill. There was nothing to be done about it. Lee Brown relaxed, his throat opened, and though his voice was quiet, it was firm. "Why do you want to kill me, son? I'm just an old man. What pride is there in killing an old man?"

The gun popped. Once. Twice. Lee Brown felt no pain, rather a tug at his thin shoulder and a tap on one side of his skull. His knees buckled and the world around him seemed to slow down.

▼ ▼ ▼

Like so many in the neighborhood, Lee Brown's children had moved to large houses in suburban towns. After his wife died, he had tried living with the children. First with Elena in her long ranch house. For a week or so, he'd enjoyed exploring the house. It had three bathrooms. He had raised his family with one small bathroom and he had grown up with an outhouse. But soon he became bored with Elena's beautiful house and began to wander her neighborhood. Here the houses were well kept, the lawns were neat, and the hedges were trimmed. He was surprised that many of the neighbors were black and that they often had friendly smiles or nods for him. Yet there was something cold about the long, brick houses and shady lawns. He had no passion for these homes. They were not Howard Square.

His son Harry lived in a newer, even more alien subdivision. His house was as big as Elena's, only it was tall with steep gables and Palladian windows. It looked the same as all the other houses, and the streets seemed to be arranged in patterns of curlicues, so that every time he went for a walk, he got lost. He begged to return to Howard Square, and eventually his children gave in.

Now he visited them only on holidays. Last Christmas they had met at Elena's house for dinner. He sat in the living room in front of the towering fieldstone fireplace. Todd sat across from him on the sofa. He was engrossed in a novel. The boy's delicate features were unlike any other in Lee Brown's family, a trait the boy's divorced mother had given him. Often Lee Brown tried to talk to the boy about the old days in Howard Square, but Todd was always preoccupied. Lee Brown felt he was talking to himself. Finally, Lee Brown took pleasure in simply looking at his grandson. He loved to watch the boy work on those weekends when he came to help his father. He especially liked to watch Todd paint. The boy painted in lazy, graceful strokes. Lee Brown thought of him as an orchestra conductor. Oh, if he could only paint up all of this old neighborhood, Lee Brown thought.

His children's voices carried from the kitchen. "They must think I'm deafer than I am," Lee Brown smiled to himself.

"Why do you allow him to live in that squalor?" Silvie's smoker's voice was histrionic as usual.

"You don't know what we go through with him," Elena answered. Lee Brown imagined she cast her eyes upward to stay her anger. "You aren't here to worry about him from day to day."

"I do have my career—"

"Sis," Harry broke in. "He's comfortable there. It's all he knows. You bring him out here, and he's lost." It would take a man to understand, Lee Brown thought.

"Comfortable! In the slums!"

"It's not the slums," Elena broke in. "It's where you grew up." Yes, Lee Brown thought. It was where you were raised, girl. He remembered that Silvie was just a baby when they moved to Howard Square. Images of Silvie growing up flashed through his mind. He had had such high hopes for her.

"I did not grow up in the slums!"

"It wasn't the slums when we grew up there," Harry said. "He remembers it the old way, as a quaint little neighborhood. He doesn't know anything else." For Pete's sake, Lee Brown thought, I know more things than that boy can count. "After all," Harry continued, "many things have changed since he was young."

Lee Brown looked at his grandson. Such a strange boy. Always deep in thought. His body was in this world, but his mind was elsewhere. He wore an earring, a simple gold hoop. It had been a long time since Lee Brown had seen an earring like that on a man. When he was a child in the 1920s, a few of the very old men, the ones with Creek blood, had worn earrings. Perhaps his grandson would understand what his own children had missed. After all, it seemed Todd was an artist.

The talk in the kitchen became quiet; perhaps the children remembered that he was just down the hall. Then Harry walked through the room, apparently talking to himself. "Best thing that could happen would be if a developer tore it down and turned it into a shopping mall."

It took a moment for Lee Brown to realize that Harry meant Howard Square. "What did he say?" he asked Todd. The boy looked up, shrugged, looked back at his book. Lee Brown turned abruptly to the fireplace. "I'd as soon burn it down."

"You said something, Daddy?" Elena came into the room with a tray of crackers and cheese.

"I'd burn it down first."

"Burn what down, Daddy?" Elena set the tray on the coffee table and bent over to look at him. "My God, your face is red. Daddy, are you all right?"

"I'm fine. Stop fussing over me, for Pete's sake."

Silvie made an entrance. "Fussing over you? Darling, that's what we're supposed to do!" She fluffed a pillow and tried to push it behind his shoulders.

"For Pete's sake, girl, if I wanted a pillow don't you think I could get one for myself?"

Elena gave Silvie a knowing nod. "Now, Daddy, Silvie was just trying to make you comfy. That's what we all want, for you to be happy."

Lee Brown wanted to say something mean to his daughters, but he knew Elena was right. "I am happy." He let out a long irritated sigh. "But I would be happier if you would just leave me alone."

"Oh, Daddy, you don't mean that," Elena said and walked back to the kitchen. "If it weren't for us, what would you do? You couldn't even feed yourself."

Silvie sat on the sofa next to Todd. She lit a cigarette and took a long drag. "Daddy, why are you such an irascible old darling? Why don't you come up to New York and live with me? It's not the same as living out here, you know. It's the city. More like what you're used to."

"And what would I do in New York, daughter? I don't know anybody in New York City."

"You could get to know someone. There's a darling old widow who lives in my building. I bet you and she would get along just fine."

"The idea of *you* playing matchmaker for me!" He shook his head. "I still can't count the number of husbands you've had."

"I've only had two." She turned on one hip, knees facing Todd. "And a couple of friends. But, Daddy, that's really unfair. I'm only trying to take care of you."

"I appreciate that. But I don't see how you can take care of yourself, much less me. What am I supposed to do, cooped up in some tiny apartment fifty stories up in the air? I'd die."

"Well, I'm sorry if I couldn't accommodate you." She rested the hand with the cigarette against her cheek and stared at Todd for a moment. "What you reading, baby?" Her voice crackled, and Lee Brown could tell she was trying not to cry. Todd held up the cover of the book for her and went back to reading.

"Honey…" Lee Brown paused. He wanted to chastise her, but he didn't want to argue. What had she been doing in New York City all this time? Hadn't he worked hard to see that she had gotten a good education? "Honey, I've worked hard all my life to see to it that—"

She faced him, tears running down her cheeks. "Don't lecture, Daddy. I know I've disappointed you. Everybody can't be a professor or an executive. Some of us fall flat on our faces no matter how hard we try. You just don't know. You are stuck in your little world of yesterday. You don't know how hard it is today." She turned to Todd. "Todd can tell you." Todd did not look up from his book.

"Todd doesn't need to tell me; I ain't dead." Lee Brown shifted forward in his chair. "Today is always harder than yesterday. For better or for worse, yesterday's gone and today is staring you right in the face."

Silvie's eyes widened. It was a look both fearful and amazed. Suddenly Lee Brown remembered the same look on Silvie's face from decades before, when she was a teenager. He had driven the family to Montgomery to witness the Selma marchers. They had left Atlanta before dawn and met up with the marchers south of Montgomery in the late morning. They parked along the side of the road with other spectators who watched in silent reverence as the marchers went by. Gloria refused to let the children get out of the car for fear they might get shot. But Silvie, arguing that her age gave her privilege, stood outside the car with him. In two long columns the marchers filed by. Some of them were singing. Some carried slogans. They were mostly black, but many whites were among them. Some wore undershirts and bib overalls. Some wore shirt and tie, or Sunday dresses. There were nuns in habits and college kids in jeans and sneakers.

Toward the end of the columns hobbled a white man with one leg missing below the knee. He seemed oblivious to his hardship as he leaned on his crutches and swung his good leg ahead of him. When he had passed, Lee Brown saw the look in Silvie's eyes.

"What is he doing?" she asked.

"He's marching."

She looked after the man and then back at her father. "Then I'm going to march, too." Lee Brown was both amused and proud. He took his daughter's hand, fell in at the end of the columns, and walked five miles.

The memory made Lee Brown smile. "Silvie, you could always accommodate me. Now, I've got a good idea that might help both of us. Why don't you come back to Howard Square?"

Silvie straightened and looked surprised. "But, Daddy…I have my career. Besides, you've spoiled me. I could never be happy there again."

Lee Brown shook his head. "Spoiled you? What the dickens are you talking about?"

Silvie dragged on her cigarette. "You made us want better things than Howard Square could offer. You made us want to make something big out of ourselves. That's what I want to do, Dad—and I'm still going to do it. I am never going back to Howard Square. As far as I'm concerned, it doesn't exist anymore. It's dead."

Lee Brown sat back in his chair. He looked about the room full of polished furniture and leather chairs. Decorated with Christmas greenery and candles, the room imparted a warmth he could no longer achieve in Howard Square. Perhaps she was right. Howard Square was dead. Gloria was dead. Most of his old neighbors were dead. So why wouldn't Howard Square be dead?

After supper, Silvie sang along with Christmas songs on a Nat King Cole album. Lee Brown closed his eyes. What a voice! he thought. He felt ashamed he had ever asked her to come back to Howard Square.

▼ ▼ ▼

He was lying on the floor between the counter and the shelves. Around him voices were swimming, but he couldn't see anyone. He heard plainly what they were saying, but he couldn't put the words into context. Who is dead? Not him. He tried to move, but there was that voice again, Elena saying, "Daddy, you take your medicine? You didn't forget to take your medicine, did you?" Now he was being dragged. Why would anyone drag him, and why would he allow it? Just lie out flat and limp as a flounder and allow it?

"I told you not to shoot the motherfucker," a voice was saying. "I told you he wasn't going to talk."

"Better safe than sorry. Here, put him on ice."

"What?"

"Put him on ice. Hide him in here. Longer it take them to find him, more time we got."

Lee Brown heard a racket. Someone was tearing up his store. Cans were falling, rolling around on the floor. Who was tearing up his store?

"In there?"

"Put him on ice," the voice said, and Lee heard a nervous, girlish "Heh, heh, heh."

"He dead. What you got to do that for?"

"I told you to hide him. Give us more time."

"Ain't nobody coming in here!"

"We hide him and put the closed sign on the door. Then make sure nobody come in here."

Now Lee Brown felt himself being lifted. His body was being pushed into a cold smooth space. The coldness chilled him and he shivered. He opened his eyes and saw the white enamel inside of the refrigerator. This was the one he'd kept drinks in for thirty years. He twisted his body, trying to straighten out, but the boys pushed him further into the space.

"He still 'live," came a surprised voice. Precious' grandson. He remembered when he first saw the boy. What was his name? LeShawn? LeMar? Something with Le on it. He turned and reached for the boy. For a second he thought the boy was reaching back for him. For a second he thought he saw mercy in the boy's face. He had seen mercy many times. Generally people were brimming over with mercy. Mercy for hungry stray cats. Mercy for the birds fallen from the nest. Occasionally even mercy for another person. But when mercy came to you, it looked different. It did not look kind. It looked all-powerful.

Then the plump boy pushed Precious' grandson aside. "You brought this on yourself, Grandpa." He pointed the gun and fired. The bullet nipped Lee Brown's ear. He felt himself go limp; his arm fell against the floor. The plump boy tucked the arm against Lee Brown's body and shut the refrigerator door. The refrigerator's motor came on.

In the box, Lee Brown could only hear the hum of the motor. He lay still for awhile, listening to it. It was a lullaby. His eyes were burning; he wanted to sleep. Slowly he realized that he mustn't sleep. He opened his eyes. The burning was caused by blood, running into his eye. He felt a graze on the side of his head. That was the bleeder. Next to it was a wound to his ear. He could only feel the bottom part of the lobe. Damn that boy. When I get out of here…

His legs were pushed up into the air, so he shifted until he was sitting on his rump. That was more comfortable, though now there was a burning in his shoulder. He was bent forward but couldn't feel the wound. It seemed high and in the fleshy part of his shoulder. That boy couldn't hit a brick wall.

▼ ▼ ▼

Before Christmas dinner, he and Harry had taken a stroll out onto the patio that overlooked a man-made lake. The day was overcast and humid, and the color of the muddy lake was not too different from that of the sky. Harry had given him a bourbon on ice and had winked. It would be their secret from Elena, who worried that he should not drink on top of his medication.

"Dad." Harry shook the ice in his glass and sipped. "The girls and I have been talking, and we think it's time that you stayed with one of us again." He held up an index finger to indicate he was not through. "I know we've tried this before and that the store means a lot to you. But I think we can work something out. Maybe if we let you keep the store on certain days. Maybe Saturdays. You live with one of us during the week."

"You know how I feel about living out here."

"It's not just about how you feel anymore. It's about your safety. The city just isn't safe anymore. Just last week somebody got killed not three blocks from the store."

"It was a kid." Lee Brown didn't know the kid but imagined he must have been the one he had seen slumped against a telephone pole, looking out for the police so that drug dealers could work.

"If they would kill a child, what wouldn't they do to you?"

Lee Brown sipped. "Life is dangerous all around, son. I know you all want to look out for me, and I thank God I raised children as good as you all. But Howard Square is not just my home. It's grown into me. I helped to build it." Looking at Harry was like looking at a younger version of himself. He hoped that Harry would understand that Howard Square was more than just boards and bricks to him. "It helped to build me. And you, too. Do you think you and Elena would live in these big fine houses if you hadn't lived in Howard Square first? You went to school there. You went to church there. You were raised there, and it raised you up."

"You don't have to preach, Dad. I know where I come from. I know that you put in your time in Howard Square. Now, it's time for you to take your reward."

"What reward?"

"Your rest."

"You mean die?"

"No, Dad, I mean rest. Retire. Relax." Harry downed his drink.

"Retire? It's not something I can retire from, son. It's my life."

"Listen to yourself. Howard Square is not your life. It's a place. It's a place we outgrew long ago. You can romanticize it, but you don't have to live there." His voice was becoming an intense whisper. "You made Mom live there until she died, but you don't have to die there."

Lee Brown gripped the glass tightly. He wanted to bang it on the patio railing or throw it to the ground. "Your mother *loved* Howard Square as much as I did."

Harry looked at the lake. His eyes squinted like he was looking for something on the lake. "I'm sure Mom did love it."

"She loved it because she loved you." He took a breath and thought twice about saying what he wanted to say. Then he said it. "You don't understand with what spite you repay her."

Harry looked at him and shook his head with surprise. "It's a slum, Dad. Your work there is over."

▼ ▼ ▼

He awoke from the dream with alarm. The cold was beginning to make his joints ache. His shoulder was throbbing. He mustered his strength, twisted his torso so that he could put both palms against the refrigerator door. He pushed. It was an old refrigerator with the kind of handle that hooked the door shut rather than the newer kind that held the door with a magnet. He pushed again, so hard that he groaned. Then he gasped. His stomach cramped and he could only take in short breaths of the moldy air because of his twisted position.

Slowly he realized that there was light, just a thread coming from behind him and reflecting off the white enamel surface. With difficulty he turned his body so that he could see where the light was coming from. A small hole. Perhaps where the bullet had gone through the back of the refrigerator. This gave him courage. He had air and light. As long as he had air, he wouldn't die. He turned again and tried to place his feet against the inside of the door. Try as he might, he could only get one foot in a position. He pushed. A crack appeared around the door seal. Thank Jesus, he thought. With just a little more strength he could break the door. His leg began to quiver and his foot ached. The crack widened a little, but the door held. His leg trembled so badly that he had to rest, but when he stopped pushing, the crack did not close all the way. Thank God. He would get out. All he needed was to take his time. His exertion made him warm and he broke into a sweat.

▼ ▼ ▼

What had that boy meant by "You brought this on yourself?" It seemed now to Lee Brown that the boy had the air of a sentencing judge. Arrogant. He wouldn't have allowed such arrogance from one of his own. Any child of his who acted that arrogantly would have gotten a backhand. Though he had threatened many times, he had never struck any of his children. He had whipped them plenty. He had a special belt for that. That's all Precious' grandson really needed, a good whipping. He remembered that he had said that to Precious when they had talked about her grandson.

"It's kinda hard for his Daddy to whip from the jailhouse," Precious had said and looked away from him as she rocked her chair. Her rocking was a language all its own, and over the years Lee Brown had learned to read it. The two strong abrupt movements meant she was frustrated. Next she would turn to him and say something about her troubles and ask him rhetorically what she could do about them. "I'm an old woman. He don't listen to me. I might as well be talking to the wind." She looked up at him. The chair was still. "Sometimes…sometimes I'm just scared of him."

Lee Brown clenched his fist. "You don't mean he'd hurt you?"

Precious rocked nervously, short movements that started with her head and shoulder. "What you gone do about it, Lee? You're old too."

"I'm not so old that I would take trash from a boy—"

"Yes, you are."

He unclenched his fist and let his hands lie limply in his lap. If the boy had come up to him at that moment and slapped him, he could have done no more than fall to the floor. He felt weak; but worse, he felt worthless.

Precious started talking again, quietly and nervously. "I wish I hadn't had those children now. I wouldn't have the worry. My oldest—I believe he would have made good if he had lived. But all the rest of them have just given me misery, Mr. Brown. You work so hard to do right by them. Give them everything you can. All you get is misery out of them. Just misery." She was calling him Mr. Brown rather than Lee, so he knew she was just feeling sorry for herself, not making a confession. "Your children, too. I know they made good where mine didn't, but still what you got, Lee? What you got now that you're old?"

Lee Brown looked down the street at the rows of dilapidated houses. He imagined how they had looked in their heyday when they were painted bright colors and neatly dressed children walked with their schoolbooks to the corner for the bus. He missed the way things were. But he hadn't lost anything, he thought. He had three children who loved him. They didn't love Howard Square, but they hadn't built Howard Square, either. He started to say that to Precious, but he thought that would be too mean to say. All she had was a caseworker. "Precious," he said after a long sigh, "what choice did we have?"

▼ ▼ ▼

The plump boy was wrong. He hadn't brought this on himself. He had done his part. He was still doing his part. Precious was still doing her part, too. They could do no more than that, regardless of what crazy bent the world took. He pushed the door again. This time he failed to widen the crack. His leg trembled. He was putting forth great effort, and nothing was happening. He couldn't feel his legs anymore; they were falling asleep. He hated when that happened, when his arms and legs became limp and useless. He shifted again, a tingling came into one leg, but the other was still dead. Jesus, have mercy. He began to count his blessings. He had air. That was the important thing. He wasn't bleeding much. He could deal with the limp limbs if he moved every now and again. The cold was bad, but it wouldn't get colder than about 40 degrees. That's no worse than a cool fall day. All he had to do was to wait. Soon Elena, his baby girl, would come looking for him. She wouldn't find him at home and would come to the store. His sweet, sweet baby girl. Thank God.

▼ ▼ ▼

He was dreaming again: it was not Elena who opened the door but Silvie. Every day she looked more like her mother. "You look no worse for the wear," Silvie said.

"Daughter," he exclaimed, "what the hell are you doing here?"

"Just come to see my daddy," she said. "That's all. Nothing else, Daddy. Just come to see you." They hugged. Then he remembered Precious' grandson. He was suddenly angry. He got the gun from behind the counter and walked up the street to Precious' house. It was evening, and the shadows were long and soft. The sunlight on the sides of the houses had a tint of rose that made the buildings seem newly painted. Precious stood up to greet him as he climbed the stairs to her porch. "Can I help you, Mr. Brown?" she asked.

"That damn grandboy of yours. LeMar? Where is he?"

"What you want with—?"

"Here I am." LeMar came to the screen door. "What do you want, old man?"

"Come here. I want you."

LeMar stepped through the screen door and Lee Brown raised and aimed the pistol. The boy's face was smooth, with just the suggestion of a mustache. His eyes were round and fearful. The fear, though, was not the fear of the gun, Lee Brown realized. The boy had seen a gun before. It was the fear that all boys have when they realize they are about to become men and must discover what that means.

Lee Brown put the gun in his pocket. "Come here, boy. Closer." The boy took a step closer. Old Lee Brown raised up his arms to embrace him.

# Rocket 88

On this visit home, I realize that my parents have grown old. My mother, Isabel, has lost thirty pounds since I last saw her. The doctor told her she needed to in order to check her diabetes. Without the weight she looks frail and a little stooped. Her temples are white, even with the henna wash she has colored her hair with. She is wearing a belted sundress and flat-laced shoes, and I think how this outfit emphasizes her age. On the other hand, there is nothing frail about my father Bill. He has put on a little paunch and wears it well, considering his six-foot-plus frame. He has not gone bald evenly, and his head has patches of white and bald. This time for the first time, I learn that they have begun sleeping in separate bedrooms.

My family has gathered at the recreation shelter on the grounds of the nuclear power plant where my sister works. We are celebrating my grandparents' sixtieth wedding anniversary. The shelter, a metal roof on columns with picnic tables under it, is on a peninsula on a lake. Just the tops of the concrete reactor domes show through the haze above the pines. My mother calls everyone to attention, and my various uncles, aunts, and cousins, about thirty in all, finally hush and gather around. She sits atop a picnic table and swings her feet as she reads them the safety rules so that they will know, as she says, what to expect should they drown. Linda, my wife of three years, elbows me. "We ought to be taping this." Every time she hears my mother make a speech, she says that.

Mom tells the story of how Grandpa and Grandma met. She begins by saying it was in 1990 and, after the giggles, corrects herself and says 1930. It was during the harvest, when Grandpa was a field hand for Grandma's grandpa. She tells about how shy Grandma was. Grandma hides her face with her hands and everybody laughs. Grandpa looks confused, then uncomfortable. Grandma tries to explain to him, and he shakes his full head of white hair. Then Mom repeats herself, "Shy, Daddy. Momma was too shy to have supper with you that first night."

"Oh," my grandfather says but doesn't seem to understand.

"Then Grandma's grandmother, who is my *great*-grandmother, said, 'Nancy, you'd better catch that fellow. He's a nice one.' " Again there is laughter. "On the next evening Daddy came and serenaded her with an old guitar."

"Serenade?" my brother-in-law Glenn asks. He is holding my nephew, Callie, five years old. "You mean like *sing?*"

"Sang and played the guitar," my mother says. "Of course, *you* wouldn't know about that. You young people wouldn't. But they used to court that way long ago."

"Yes, indeed," my Great-uncle Reed says. "Jim had a nice voice, too. Could sing 'Deep River' and 'She'll Be Comin' Round the Mountain'. " He slapped his hand on his knee.

"What about you, Momma?" my sister Tracie asks. "Did Daddy sing to you?"

My mother shook her head, and my father, from the back of the group says, "Y'all off the subject. It ain't my anniversary."

My mother and her sister have made a display of family photographs going back several generations. There are battered pictures of my great-grandparents, an old farm couple standing as grim as *American Gothic.* There are many baby pictures, especially of my cousins and my sister and myself. Some of these bear my mother's trademark of photographing us naked while we lay belly-flat on a diaper. One photograph catches my eye. It is a picture of my parents when they were young. My father is encircling my mother's waist and they are leaning against a sedan with a high rounded roof and rounded fenders. Behind the front tire, beside my father's outstretched legs, is an emblem. I make it out to read "Rocket 88."

In the photograph my mother is wearing a white belted sundress and flat buckled shoes. She is slim but not frail. My father's skin appears exceptionally smooth. He wears a razor-thin mustache and a half-grin that makes him look both charming and a little foolish. My mother looks directly at the camera and smiles demurely.

My mother's sister, Aunt Tee, is sitting nearby with her husband, Uncle Simms. I ask her about the photograph. She says she remembers when the photo was taken, that it was 1950 or so, about a year before my parents were married. She remembers this, she says, because of the car. "Isabel loved to see that old car coming, and Bill would always have it polished so bright for her. But it was always muddy before they got off the yard—it being the country." She says how she hates the country and how she wishes she still lived in the city. But Popsy, as she calls Uncle Simms, had to retire to the country and make her leave all of her beautiful things in the city. She tells about her house in Montclair, New Jersey, just twenty minutes from downtown Manhattan. She had to sell much of her furniture and china when they moved into the smaller house, and she misses those things. She sighs. "Well, I say it wasn't my house anyway. It was God's. That's my philosophy. I was just using it until I passed on to glory. It's somebody else's to use now."

Uncle Simms, sick with emphysema, sucks on his unlit cigarette and lets out his breath slowly. His eyes are bulging and red-rimmed. He clears his throat and looks nonchalantly at the horizon of the lake. "Any way the wind blows," he says, "it blows cold to me."

At dinner Linda and I sit with my cousin Marsha and her husband Gordon. Marsha is complaining about the heat and says she wishes we had held the picnic indoors. Gordon, his mouth full of mustard potato salad, says that the heat is good for you. "Sweatin's good 'cause it cleans out your system." Linda gives me the eye. She thinks all my relatives are crazy. I tell her they are just relaxed, and if you can't relax with relatives, whom can you relax with?

"But the sun's too dag hot," Marsha says. "It's making me black, and I don't need to get any blacker." Marsha is the darkest one in our family. It's not talked about much, but Uncle Simms is not her real father. She was conceived before Aunt Tee and Uncle Simms were married, but she was born after the marriage, and Uncle Simms has treated her just like his own. My grandmother says she doesn't understand how a man can just leave his own child, never even see it once. She can understand how people can get divorced, even though it's not scriptural. But she could never in a thousand years see how a person could desert his own flesh and blood.

Marsha and Gordon have been married eight years and have a seven-year-old named Candee. She took her father's coloring and her mother's looks. We think this is a blessing.

"Do you know what is the best thing for you?" Gordon asks Linda.

She says no, looks at me and takes a tiny bite of chicken breast.

"The very best thing in the world. It will fix anything that's wrong with you, and if you eat it all the time, nothing will ever go wrong with you."

"Dag," Marsha says, "not that again."

"But *you* eat it, don't you?"

"With you talking all the time, what choice do I have?" Marsha looks at me and gives me her pretty smile. We share a secret laugh at Gordon.

"Oatmeal," Gordon says. "Oatmeal will fix anything. Like I was overweight last year and I went on an oatmeal diet. I'm gonna write a diet book about it. *The Oatmeal Diet.* It's a miracle food, because it's got fourteen of the essential vitamins—plus roughage—and what it ain't got, vitamin D milk's got. All together it's twenty-one kinds of vitamins. If you get that twenty-one then nothing will go wrong with you."

"You've got that bald spot coming," I say. "Maybe I ought to smear some *oatmeal* on it."

Gordon looks flustered for a moment. "Go ahead and laugh now," he says, "but by the time you are Grandma and Grandpa's age you will probably be dead and I will be as healthy as I want to be."

I get up to get another hot dog from the grill and Linda follows me. "How the hell does she stand living with him?" she asks. I shrug and look back at them. Marsha is feeding Gordon a piece of rib and laughing as the barbecue sauce drips on him. At the table next to them my mother sits with Aunt Tee and Uncle Simms, who still holds his unlit cigarette. My grandparents sit at the head table with Uncle Reed, whose wife and children were killed long before I was born. Uncle Reed is bouncing Callie on his knee. My father sits almost diagonally across the shelter from my mother. Tracie and Glenn are at the table with him.

My father has been retired for a year from air-conditioning repair. He says he has always hated air conditioners, but it was good money. He wouldn't allow an air conditioner in the house. All the years they shared a bedroom, he wouldn't even allow my mother to run a window fan. He believes night breezes are unhealthy. The house is so hot that when Linda and I visit in the summer, we stay at a nearby motel. After my mother changed rooms, she put a window unit in her bedroom. When I first saw the separate bedrooms, I thought it was funny. I thought my father's eccentricity had finally gotten the best of her. Now, as I watch them at the picnic, I slowly realize the problem is much deeper.

After dinner Aunt Tee brings out a tiered wedding cake with a little bride and groom on top of it. Everybody gathers round while Grandma and Grandpa cut the cake, and Tracie poses them feeding it to each other. Glenn opens bottles of sparkling apple cider and tells everybody it is champagne for the toast. I am standing next to my father, and my mother is at the front of the shelter cutting slices of cake. Uncle Reed is called upon for the toast. He lifts his plastic glass and smiles widely, showing his straight but dingy teeth. "I make this toast," he says, "to the best couple I know. For sixty years…" His smile drops and his hand trembles a little. Aunt Tee steps in behind him and puts a hand on his shoulder. He smiles again, briefly, "For sixty wonderful years…" His face contorts and he apologizes and says, "All the best," sits down, and covers his eyes with his free hand. Everyone stares silently, except Grandpa who is confused and looking about for an explanation. Then my father raises his glass and says, "Hear, hear," and like it is some vintage movie, we all raise our glasses and say, "Hear, hear," and drink the cider. I gulp mine down too fast; it burns my nose and I almost choke. I feel Dad pat me between the shoulder blades, and I see Mom look up from slicing the cake. For a moment I feel six years old, and I want both of my parents by my side at the same time.

Dad takes his cake and returns to the far table. I join him and ask him about the Rocket 88. For a moment he looks like he doesn't know what I'm talking about, then his brown eyes light up and he rubs his hand across his patchy head. "Damn. That old Oldsmobile. It was my first. My first damn car. It was new, you know—but I didn't buy it new. I took up the payments when Uncle Henry was lost in Korea. She was a beaut. A real treasure." He explained the engine configuration on the car. It was 1951, and the company had just gone to the V-8 with this model in 1949. Some were called Futura 88s, but this one was called a Rocket. "It was like a rocket to the moon. I'd polish her up every weekend and go get your momma, and we would just ride and talk, and ride and talk. We never really went anywhere, but it seemed, driving down those old roads, that we were going to the end of the world. I always loved a good drive." He chewed his cake absently for a moment. "In those days, you see, we thought nothing would ever go wrong. There was the war, and Henry and all, but your momma and me..." He scratched at the gray stubble on his cheeks. "Hell, sometimes an old car just fizzles out."

▼ ▼ ▼

My mother and I are strolling along the path that leads from the shelter down to the beach when Tracie, Glenn, and Callie catch up to us. Glenn is carrying a yellow air mattress under his arm and Callie on his shoulders. Tracie, who has gained two pounds for every one my mother has lost, has changed into a flower-print bathing suit with a matching cover-up. I want to say something about how awful she looks, but she smiles and gives me a playful tug on the ear.

"Whaddaya say, mule ears," she calls me by a childhood name.

"Whale butt" or "elephant thigh" would be appropriate responses, but I cannot be this cruel. Instead, I denigrate myself by saying how my ears will grow even more once I get into the radioactive waters of the lake. Glenn laughs and turns the teasing back on Tracie. He calls her an environmental villain for working at a nuclear power plant, though she is only a secretary. She reminds him that his work isn't so environmentally safe either, as he is a chemical engineer. She says that his company dumps more poison in one hour into the river that feeds the lake than the plant would in twenty years. Glenn corrupts the power company's motto: "We bring 'new' things to life." He says that his company only kills the fish, but hers mutates them. Callie squirms down from Glenn's shoulders and pulls his parents by the hands to hurry them to the beach.

When they are ahead, my mother says how awful it is that they joke about pollution. Her eyes seem watery as though from allergies or a cold. She looks tired. "The world is just falling apart. Used to be you never heard of pollution or mutation, not in these parts anyway. You wouldn't worry about swimming in a lake."

"If you're worried...," I start, "but I think it's safe."

"We couldn't stop them anyway. They're all excited about swimming. Little Callie has been talking about it all week."

She pauses and leans against the trunk of a young pine. Across a finger of the lake we can see the reactor domes, two sand-colored globes set in a platform of concrete. "In a way, they are pretty," she says.

"Tell me something, Mom," I say, "tell me about that picture of you and Dad and the Rocket 88."

"What do you want to know?" She doesn't look at me. She doesn't seem surprised that I am asking.

"I don't know...just something...I mean, you look so young."

"We were young. I was eighteen or nineteen. He may have been twenty."

"Did you love him?" I ask. I swallow hard. It is not the question I need to ask.

She smiles a little, but it is not a nostalgic smile; it is a comforting smile for me. "Of course we were in love." She glances at the reactors and then back to me. "You are still a little boy, older than I was when I had you, but still my little boy." She touches my ear, not with a tug like Tracie, but more of a caress. "But that's not what you really want to know." I shake my head no, and she does not make me ask her. "I respect your father. He is a sweet man, always has been. But I don't *love* him anymore." She looks back at the domes. "I don't remember when I stopped or when I realized it exactly." She starts to walk again. "Just one day I realized I was more comfortable sleeping with the air conditioner."

"But...did he do something to you? I mean..."

She stops and touches my elbow. "No, my boy. Nothing like that. Nothing I can explain to you."

The dry pine needles crunch underfoot. I want to ask her if she will ever leave my father, but this question is too hard to me. Mom smiles. She seems to read my thoughts. "I would air-condition the whole house if I could. But now that your father has retired, I can't afford it."

We come out of the pine woods onto a tiny strip of sand at the lake's edge. Mom holds my hand and pats it. "People don't always work out like your grandma and grandpa. But whatever, in good families, the children never suffer." Suddenly she squeezes my hand as if surprised and gives me a questioning look. "No, that's not true. But we never *intend* for them to suffer."

"I'm not suffering," I say. I want so desperately to see my parents side by side. To see them lean against that old Rocket 88 and smile as in the photograph. I try to think of the last time I saw them together, relaxed and happy with each other. I can't.

I stop. She walks a step, stops and turns. For a moment sadness brings me to the brink of tears. "Mom," I say. I struggle to form the question, the one I want her to answer in the affirmative, even if it is a lie. "Mom, won't you even try?"

"Try? I have tried. Very hard." Her cheek trembles, and she forces a smile. "You don't see it now because you're so young. Love is bigger than you've ever imagined, but it isn't everything. It can't do everything."

"I only want it to do *one* thing," I say.

She drops my hand. "For whom? For you or for me?" She shakes her head. "Never mind. Don't answer that." She has come to the end of her patience. “I love you. Your father loves you. You have a beautiful wife who loves you.” She takes a step away, hesitates. “You can have the photograph,” she says and goes to help Aunt Tee who is situating my grandparents on blankets.

▼ ▼ ▼

The water is green in spite of the sandy bottom. In the shallows it is only slightly cooler than the air, but refreshing nonetheless. I push off, eyes closed, and feel the water glide around me. I bump against the safety rope and dive under. Suddenly the water becomes chilly and I realize that just beyond the rope is a drop-off into deep water. My father looks up at me and I think for a moment that he will give me his famous arm’s-length “come-on-in” beckon, the one he gave us when we were children. But he only stares and then turns back to his conversation with Uncle Reed.

I aim for a buoy a couple hundred yards out. As I stroke and breathe, I can see the receding shoreline through my water-beaded eyelashes. Each stroke is taking me further away from my family. The swimming feels good, and I think I won’t stop at the buoy but swim to the other side of the lake. Then I realize I am halfway between the shore and the buoy, skimming the surface of cold green water of unknown depth.

After my swim, Tracie and Glenn ask if I will keep an eye on Callie while they go get changed. Callie and Candee are paddling on the air mattress near the safety rope. I begin to make my way over to them. A corner of the mattress is over the rope, so I call to Candee to stop paddling and turn around. She calls back that she is a good swimmer and continues to paddle.

“Come back from the rope,” I call again to Candee.

“My mommie lets me go over there if I want to.”

"I'm not your mommie."

"I'll say!"

"The little bitch," I say to myself.

Flaunting my warning, Candee encourages Callie to kick so the mattress can go all the way over the rope. Suddenly, Callie slips from the mattress. His head goes under the water, and his little hand grabs for the mattress and misses. Time seems to slow, though I am swimming as fast as I can. As I swim, I see my father is already running toward the water. When I get to the spot, Candee is holding onto the rope. I don't see Callie. I dive and can see nothing in the murky green. Frantically I grope in the cold, touching nothing but sand. I burst through the surface, sucking in both air and water. My father, knee-deep in the water, is still running toward us. He shouts and points just ahead of me. I see Callie's red trunks and dive for them. I catch him by the waist and lift him into the air.

A moment later, I have a footing and am carrying him toward the shore. He is coughing and I realize he is all right. Before I get to the shore, my father takes him from me, and before he gets to shore, my mother, her dress wet and clinging to her thighs, takes him from Dad. The family begins to make a circle around Dad and Mom and Callie.

Then I see what I am hoping for, my parents standing together. She is holding the crying Callie against her shoulder. My father puts his arms around her waist. She looks at him and I think for a moment of the Rocket 88 jetting down the country roads beneath the shadowy oaks.

"He's all right," my mother announces. "Just scared." She pushes my father's arm away.

▼ ▼ ▼

Linda is driving us back to the motel on a winding, two-lane road that runs through the hilly countryside. After half an hour, pastures and woodlands give way to a large housing development under construction. The trees have been pushed aside for the development. The earth is red, scraped bare of all vegetation. The house frames dot the hillsides in perfect rows. The sunlight throws the shadows of the frames across the ground.

I break the silence we have maintained since we left the picnic. "Now there's a lovely place to live."

Linda glances at the development, then at me. "Not on your life. Too close to your crazy family."

"Lay off my family. Besides, you're part of us, too—like it or not."

She smiles coyly. When she smiles this way, her lip curls up and shows her gum and her eyelashes flutter a little. Her voice registers deeper than usual. "Well, I don't like it. Not one bit."

"What do you mean?" I flirt back. "You don't like me?"

"Maybe I do, maybe I don't. Time will tell."

"About the time it takes to get to the motel." We laugh. I kiss her on the side of the mouth and sit back, anticipating the sexual encounter that has been suggested. A cloud passes over the sun for a moment; there is distant thunder. I am daydreaming about the Rocket 88 traveling down the country lanes. In the daydream, Linda and I have replaced my parents. The daydream goes along pleasantly for awhile, then Linda stops the car with a jolt.

"Sorry. These stop signs just pop out of nowhere." We are at the crossroads where the motel is located. Before we can get into our room, a shower catches us. I am shirtless and still in my swimsuit, but Linda has changed to a T-shirt and shorts. We get soaked. The shirt is clinging to her body, and even though she is wearing a bra, her nipples show through. When we are inside, she starts to pull the shirt over her head, but I take her in my arms and press my lips hard against hers. It's not so much a kiss as just pushing our lips together. I draw her tightly to me. My God, I'm thinking, how I love her. I can't say what it is particularly I love about her. Her looks. Her smell. The sound of her voice. All of this, and more. She pushes back from me a little and then allows me to kiss her more gently. The kiss is very wet. My tongue moves around the inside of her mouth, twisting around her tongue. I begin to move us toward the bed, when she breaks away.

"Let me get out of these wet things." She goes into the bathroom and shuts the door. The air conditioner has made the room very cool, so I pull off the wet trunks, wrap myself in a blanket and sit on the bed. The storm makes a soothing sound, muffling the noise of the highway. At first the sound is very pleasant, and I am happy. I feel energetic and erotic. Saving Callie has a lot to do with both feelings. Everyone kept slapping me on the back and saying how wonderful I was. Glenn had come up to me and had shaken my hand. After she had recovered from her fright, Tracie had hugged me and wept. But it was something Dad said that was best of all. He was among the first to thank me. He put both hands on my shoulders and said, "I'm proud of you, son." I had started to say that I didn't have much choice; I did what I could, and I was lucky. He stopped me from talking. "You don't understand, son. I'm proud of everything you've done. You are a wonderful man." He didn't wait for me to thank him for the compliment, but turned and went away while others slapped my shoulders.

Sitting on the bed, I realize how invigorated I am by his speech. It is like a milestone has been reached, not so much a passage from boyhood to manhood but a passage to a place where my father has recognized me as a man. Now I begin to get sad. I begin to think of my father as a man who has reached a milestone as well. He has passed into old age, has passed his prime. The others had gathered around me and were laughing and slapping my back while my father walked away. His walk had a sturdy, elegant swagger, but he was a lone figure as he headed up toward the pines. Remembering the way he looked when he walked away, I realize how alone he is. He deserves better.

Linda crawls into the bed and sits beside me. "Why so gloomy?" We kiss. "What's wrong?"

"Just thinking." I lie back on the bed.

"About?"

"About love. It's strange."

"Love isn't so strange." She rubs her hand across my chest.

"Oh, yes, it is. It's very strange, if you think about it."

"Don't think about it. Not now." We kiss again. It is a long deep kiss in which I am momentarily lost in her smell and touch. When she pulls away, I try to pull her back. "Whoa, boy. Take it easy." She laughs and snuggles under the blanket with me.

"Listen," I say. We listen to the rain for a moment, to the rumbling thunder. In the still dimness, I listen to her breathe. Each breath seems to mark time. I wish that time would stand still. "I don't ever want you to leave me."

"I won't." She rolls on top of me.

"I really mean it. Don't ever leave me. I wouldn't be able to stand it."

"I told you I won't."

I grab her wrists and tense up. "Promise me."

She sits up. "Promise you what? That I won't leave you? What makes you think that I would?"

I don't have an answer right away, not one that I can articulate. I remember the look on my father's face when he talked about the Rocket 88, about driving the country roads with my mother. How perfect things must have seemed to him then. But sometimes, he said, an old car just putters out. "I don't want us to become like my parents. I don't want us to grow apart."

"I don't want to," she says. She loosens my grip and frees her wrists. "But you never can tell. Things happen…or they don't happen. Some things you can do something about, and some you can't. I believe your parents can do something about their marriage, dear. I honestly do. It may be difficult for them, but if they would only try. And if they won't, there's nothing we can do—if they won't do it for themselves." She goes to the window, pulls the draperies open a few inches, and peers out. A cool, blue light enters the room.

"But if she doesn't love him?"

"Well, if she doesn't love him, I'm sorry. Maybe it's too late."

"She doesn't love him. I asked her. She told me so."

"I'm sorry."

I sit up. "But why? How could they just stop loving each other after all these years?"

"I don't know, honey. I'm sorry."

I try to think back to a time when my parents may have grown apart. No specific incident comes to mind. No particular argument. They rarely argued. It seems that there was never a distance between them, and yet the distance must always have been there. It must have been like a crystal of ice, growing in each of them and slowly cooling them toward one another, until one day, without ceremony, my mother took a room on the other side of the house.

Linda talks softly, carefully to me. "Sometimes it's not what one or the other of them does. It's what they don't do. It's not doing the little things, and not doing the big things, too. Remember when I asked you how Marsha could stand to stay with Gordon? Well, we don't know why. We never will. I guess love is strange, but somehow they keep giving each other something. They make each other comfortable."

"And my momma and daddy don't make each other comfortable anymore?"

"I don't know. I was just talking." She shuts the curtain and comes back to the bed. She slips an arm under my neck and pulls my head toward her breasts. "You're a man. You're a baby, too. Which do you want to be tonight?"

At first I feel foolish. Have I been sounding like a baby? Then I am grateful. I realize what Linda is doing for me. I press my face against her breasts, and tears come to my eyes. For awhile, I am in a child's world, where love seems guaranteed and unconditional. I dream about the Rocket 88. The rounded fenders are gleaming in the sunlight. It is moving so smoothly over the asphalt that it seems to fly. It swoops around the curves and into the valleys. It glides through the mottled shadows in the woods and through the sunny fields. I cannot tell who is driving. It seems to be my father. It seems to be me. It seems to be my mother, and Linda, too. The road never ends. We are happy.

Anthony Grooms lives in Atlanta with his wife Pamela. He is the author of *Ice Poems*, a book of poetry from Poetry Atlanta Press. His writing has won him grants from several arts councils including The City of Atlanta Bureau of Cultural Affairs. He has been the recipient of the Sokolov Scholarship from the Bread Loaf Writers Conference and an NEA Arts Administration Fellowship. *Trouble No More* is his first book of short stories.

J. D. SCOTT